KU-714-953

Leith's Vegetarian Cookery Book

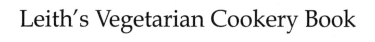

Leith's Vegetarian Cookery Book

BY
PRUE LEITH
&
CAROLINE WALDEGRAVE

First published in Great Britain 1993
Bloomsbury Publishing Limited, 2 Soho Square,
London W1V 5DE

Copyright © 1993 by Prue Leith and Caroline Waldegrave

The moral right of the authors has been asserted

A CIP catalogue record for this book
is available from the British Library

ISBN 0 7475 1233 7

10 9 8 7 6 5 4 3 2 1

Edited and designed by
Toucan Books Limited, London

Photographer: Andrea Heselton
Assisted by: Sarah Mac, Nesa Mladjenovic
Stylists: Roisin Nield, Sue Russell
Home economists: Janey Bevan, Jackie Brewer,
Puff Fairclough, Fiona Trail Stevenson, Polly Tyrer
Assisted by: Louise Bacon
Line drawings by: Kate Simunek

Printed in Great Britain by The Bath Press, Avon

Contents

Acknowledgements

This book is officially by Prue Leith and me. In fact this is not really true. Teachers, students and friends of Leith's School of Food and Wine alike have all contributed. Recipes have been unashamedly adapted from magazines, newspaper articles and other cookery books. If we can remember the original source for a recipe we have credited the person involved, but sometimes I'm afraid we no longer know where they came from and hope that their creators will forgive us.

I would particularly like to acknowledge the work of the following people: Fiona Burrell, Alison Cavaliero, Richard Harvey, C.J. Jackson, Charlotte Lyon, Sally Procter, Sarah Staughton, Barbara Stevenson, Lesley Waters and Caroline Yates.

I would also like to thank all those involved in the production of this book, particularly Robert Sackville West at Toucan Books who calmly and charmingly worked so hard on our behalf.

Caroline Waldegrave

Introduction

Neither Prue nor I is vegetarian but we both love vegetarian food and Leith's Restaurant has an excellent vegetarian menu.

At Leith's School we teach a tremendous mixture of styles and recipes. We have time-honoured classic dishes rubbing shoulders with the latest fashionable ideas. There is a fairly strong vegetarian undercurrent and we find that we are adding more and more vegetarian dishes to the course each year. We are particularly lucky to have Alison Cavaliero and Caroline Yates working at the School. They are both vegetarians and have helped us enormously.

I do hope that you enjoy cooking from this book. All the recipes for this book have been taken from *Leith's Cookery Bible*.

Caroline Waldegrave

Conversion Tables

The tables below are approximate, and do not conform in all respects to the official conversions, but we have found them convenient for cooking.

Weight

Imperial	Metric	Imperial	Metric
$1/4$oz	7-8g	$1/2$oz	15g
$3/4$oz	20g	1oz	30g
2oz	55g	3oz	85g
4oz ($1/4$lb)	110g	5oz	140g
6oz	170g	7oz	200g
8oz ($1/2$lb)	225g	9oz	255g
10oz	285g	11oz	310g
12oz ($3/4$lb)	340g	13oz	370g
14oz	400g	15oz	425g
16oz (1lb)	450g	$1^1/4$lb	560g
$1^1/2$lb	675g	2lb	900g
3lb	1.35 kg	4lb	1.8 kg
5lb	2.3 kg	6lb	2.7 kg
7lb	3.2 kg	8lb	3.6 kg
9lb	4.0 kg	10lb	4.5 kg

Liquid measures

Imperial	ml	fl oz
$1^3/4$ pints	1000 (1 litre)	35
1 pint	570	20
$3/4$ pint	425	15
$1/2$ pint	290	10
$1/3$ pint	190	6.6
$1/4$ pint (1 gill)	150	5
	56	2
2 scant tablespoons	28	1
1 teaspoon	5	

Lengths

Imperial	Metric
$1/2$in	1cm
1in	2.5cm
2in	5cm
6in	15cm
12in	30cm

Oven temperatures

°C	°F	Gas mark
70	150	$1/4$
80	175	$1/4$
100	200	$1/2$
110	225	$1/2$
130	250	1
140	275	1
150	300	2
170	325	3
180	350	4
190	375	5
200	400	6
220	425	7
230	450	8
240	475	8
250	500	9
270	525	9
290	550	9

Approximate American/European conversions

Commodity Imperial	USA	Metric	
Flour	1 cup	140g	5oz
Caster and granulated sugar	1 cup	225g	8oz
Caster and granulated sugar	2 level tablespoons	30g	1oz
Brown sugar	1 cup	170g	6oz
Butter/margarine	1 cup	225g	8oz
Sultanas/raisins	1 cup	200g	7oz
Currants	1 cup	140g	5oz
Ground almonds	1 cup	110g	4oz
Golden syrup	1 cup	340g	12oz
Uncooked rice	1 cup	200g	7oz

NOTE: In American recipes, when quantities are stated as spoons, 'level' spoons are meant. English recipes (and those in this book) call for rounded spoons except where stated otherwise. This means that 2 American tablespoons equal 1 English tablespoon.

Useful measurements

Measurement Imperial	Metric	
1 American cup	225ml	8 fl oz
1 egg	56ml	2 fl oz
1 egg white	28ml	1 fl oz
1 rounded tablespoon flour	30g	1oz
1 rounded tablespoon cornflour	30g	1oz
1 rounded tablespoon sugar	30g	1oz
2 rounded tablespoons breadcrumbs	30g	1oz

Wine quantities

Imperial	ml	fl oz
Average wine bottle	730	25
1 glass wine	100	3
1 glass port or sherry	70	2
1 glass liqueur	45	1

First Courses

Gazpacho

This recipe assumes that the cook has a blender or liquidizer.

SERVES 6
900g/2lb fresh, very ripe tomatoes, peeled
1 large mild Spanish onion
2 red peppers
1 small cucumber
1 thick slice white bread, the crust cut off
1 egg yolk
2 large garlic cloves
90ml/6 tablespoons olive oil
15ml/1 tablespoon tarragon vinegar
450g/1lb tin Italian peeled tomatoes
15ml/1 tablespoon tomato purée
freshly ground black pepper
plenty of salt (preferably sea salt)

To serve:
1 large bowl croûtons

1. Chop or dice finely a small amount of the fresh tomato, onion, red pepper, and cucumber and put in separate small bowls for garnish.

2. Roughly chop the remaining vegetables to prepare them
for the liquidizer.

3. Put the bread, egg yolk and garlic into the liquidizer. Turn it on and add the oil in a thin steady stream while the machine is running. You should end up with a thick mayonnaise-like emulsion.

4. Add the vinegar and then gradually add all the soup ingredients in batches and

blend until smooth. Then sieve the soup to remove the tomato seeds and check for flavouring.

NOTE: Gazpacho should be served icy cold with the small bowls of chopped vegetables and fried croûtons handed separately. Sometimes crushed ice is added to the soup at the last minute.

If you prefer a thinner soup, dilute it with iced water or tomato juice.

CRISP DRY WHITE

Lebanese Cucumber and Yoghurt Soup

SERVES 4
1 large cucumber, peeled
290ml/½ pint single cream
140g/5 fl oz carton yoghurt
30ml/2 tablespoons tarragon vinegar
15ml/1 tablespoon chopped mint
salt and pepper

1. Grate the cucumber coarsely.

2. Stir in the rest of the ingredients and season to taste.

3. Chill for 2 hours before serving.

NOTE: This soup may be garnished with cold croûtons; chopped chives; a spoonful of soured cream added just before serving; chopped gherkins; a few pink shrimps. It is also good flavoured with garlic.

WHITE BURGUNDY

Simple Vegetable Soup

SERVES 8
45g/1½ oz butter
225g/8oz onions, chopped
450g/1 lb carrots, chopped
225g/8oz potatoes, chopped
110g/4 oz celery, chopped
425ml/¾ pint milk
860ml/1½ pints water
salt and freshly ground black pepper

1. Melt the butter in a large heavy pan with 30ml/2 tablespoons water. Add all the chopped vegetables, stir and cover with a lid. Cook slowly until soft but not coloured, stirring occasionally. This will take about 30 minutes.

2. Add the milk and water. Season with salt and pepper and simmer, without a lid, for 15 minutes.

3. Liquidize the soup and pass through a sieve.

4. Pour into the rinsed-out saucepan. Season to taste and add water if the soup is too thick. Reheat carefully.

DRY WHITE/LIGHT RED

Leith's Restaurant's Tomato and Basil Soup

SERVES 6
2.3kg/5lb tomatoes
24 large basil leaves
170g/6oz salted butter
salt and freshly ground black pepper
85g/3oz fromage blanc

1. Make a small slit in the skin of each tomato and blanch in boiling water for 5-7 seconds. They are ready to peel when the skin starts to lift away from the knife slits. Skin, then halve the tomatoes scooping the seeds and juice into a sieve set over a bowl. Sieve the juice and reserve, then cut the tomato flesh into small strips.

2. Roughly chop all but 6 of the basil leaves. Put the tomato strips, reserved juice and chopped basil into a large deep frying pan. Add 55g/2oz of the butter and place over a medium heat, shaking the pan and stirring.

3. When the tomato strips start to break up, turn up the heat and briskly stir in the rest of the butter. When all the butter has been added, the tomatoes should be only half cooked. Season with salt and pepper.

4. Fill individual soup bowls with the tomato soup, then spoon fromage blanc into the middle of each bowl. Garnish each soup bowl with a fresh basil leaf and serve at once.

SOAVE

Artichoke Soup

SERVES 4
55g/2oz butter
1 medium onion, sliced
675g/1½lb Jerusalem artichokes
570ml/1 pint milk
570ml/1 pint water
salt and freshly ground black pepper

1. Melt the butter in a saucepan and gently cook the onion in it until soft but not coloured.

2. Peel the artichokes and leave in a bowl of cold acidulated water (water with lemon juice or vinegar added) to prevent discoloration.

3. Slice the artichokes and add to the pan. Continue cooking, covered, for about 10 minutes, giving an occasional stir.

4. Add the milk and water, season well and simmer for a further 20 minutes. Do not allow it to boil, or it will curdle.

5. Liquidize and push through a sieve. Check for seasoning – this soup needs plenty of salt and pepper.

LIGHT WHITE ALSACE

Herb Omelette Salad

SERVES 2-4

For the omelette:
5 eggs
45ml/3 tablespoons olive oil
1 tablespoon chopped parsley
salt and freshly ground black pepper

For the salad:
2 red peppers, quartered and deseeded
2 large tomatoes, peeled and cut into strips
1 cucumber, peeled, deseeded and cut into strips
1 head of lettuce
1 bunch chives, roughly chopped
12 basil leaves, chopped
10 small black olives, stoned

For the dressing:
1 garlic clove, crushed
2 anchovy fillets, mashed
5ml/1 teaspoon Dijon mustard
30ml/2 tablespoons wine vinegar
120ml/8 tablespoons olive oil
freshly ground black pepper

1. To make the omelette: in a bowl mix together the eggs, 30ml/2 tablespoons of the olive oil, the parsley, and the salt and pepper.

2. Use the remaining oil to fry the omelette. Lightly grease the base of an omelette pan. When hot, add enough of the omelette mixture to cover the base of the pan. The omelette mixture should be the thickness of a pancake. Cook the omelette for about 1 minute. Slide on to a plate to cool. Continue to cook the remaining omelette mixture.

3. When cool, cut the omelettes into thin strips.

4. Meanwhile, prepare the salad. Place the peppers under a hot grill. When charred, hold under cold running water and scrape off the skin, then cut it into 1cm/^{1}/$_2$ inch strips.

5. To prepare the dressing, mix together all the ingredients, and whizz in a liquidizer. Season.

6. Mix together all the salad ingredients, the omelette strips and the herbs. Add the dressing and toss well.

7. Pile on to a serving dish, and scatter over the black olives.

LIGHT TO MEDIUM RED

Tortilla

SERVES 4

450g/1lb floury potatoes, peeled and
*   finely sliced*
1 small onion, finely sliced
salt and freshly ground black pepper
4 eggs, beaten
oil for frying

1. Heat about 1cm/^{1}/$_2$ inch of oil in a frying pan, add the potatoes and onions, season with salt and pepper and fry slowly until soft, but not coloured. This may take up to 20 minutes.

2. Tip all the oil but for a thin film out of the pan and pour the potatoes and onion into the egg mixture. Beat, then pour the egg mixture into the pan.

3. Cook the omelette over a moderate heat until it is set and then slip on to a plate. Turn it over and put it back into the frying pan with the uncooked side down.

4. Cook for a further minute and then turn out on to a serving plate. Serve warm or cold, cut into wedges.

NOTE: Frying the potatoes from raw is the usual Spanish method. But if the potatoes are small and waxy it is better to boil them first, then slice and fry. Boiled potatoes give a light, soft omelette.

RED RIOJA

Frittata (Italian Omelette)

SERVES 2

225g/8oz red onions, sliced very finely
45ml/3 tablespoons oil
3 eggs
30g/1oz fresh Parmesan cheese, grated
salt and freshly ground black pepper
20g/³/₄oz butter

1. Cook the onions slowly in the oil until reduced in quantity, soft, and a rich golden brown colour. Tip the onions into a sieve over a bowl.

2. Beat the eggs until lightly mixed. Mix all but 3 tablespoons of the eggs with the onions, cheese, salt and pepper. Mix well.

3. Melt the butter in an 18cm/6 inch frying pan over a medium heat. When foaming, add the egg and onion mixture. Reduce the heat to very low.

4. Cook very slowly for 15 minutes. The eggs should be set and the surface runny. Pour over the reserved egg. Place under a hot grill until set but not brown. Loosen with a spatula and slide on to a round dish. Serve cut into wedges.

LIGHT CHIANTI

Quail Eggs en Croustade

SERVES 4

8 quail eggs
4 thin slices bread
unsalted butter
1 shallot, finely chopped
185g/3oz flat mushrooms, finely chopped
chopped parsley
salt and freshly ground black pepper
beurre blanc (see page 145)

1. Cut the bread in circles with a large fluted pastry cutter and press very firmly into large patty tins. Brush with melted unsalted butter. Bake at 170°C/325°F/gas mark 3 for 15 minutes. Remove from the tins, turn upside down and bake for a further 10 minutes or until crisp and lightly browned.

2. Meanwhile prepare the duxelles: cook the shallot in butter. Add the mushrooms and cook for a further 2 minutes. Boil away the liquid. Add the parsley and season to taste with salt and pepper. The mixture should be very dry.

3. Poach the quail eggs in water (break 2 eggs at a time on to a saucer and then tip carefully into the saucepan, and poach for approximately 2 minutes).

4. Divide the duxelles mixture between the croustades. Place 2 eggs on top of each and coat with the beurre blanc.

LIGHT RED

Stuffed Cream Cheese Tomatoes

SERVES 2

4 tomatoes, peeled
110g/4oz good cream cheese or sieved cheese
15ml/1 tablespoon chopped fresh mint
squeeze of lemon
1/4 garlic clove, crushed
salt and freshly ground black pepper
15ml/1 tablespoon chopped fresh parsley
French dressing (see page 136)
sprigs of watercress

1. Slice a quarter of each tomato off at the rounded end. Scoop out the flesh and seeds. Discard the seeds and coarsely chop the flesh. Leave the tomatoes to drain while making the filling.

2. Mix a little of the flesh with the cream cheese, mint, lemon, garlic and the salt and pepper.

3. Fill the hollow tomatoes with this mixture and stick the tops back at a jaunty angle. Arrange on a plate.

4. Add the parsley to the dressing and shake or mix well. Spoon this over the tomatoes, and garnish with the watercress.

5. Serve with brown bread and butter.

LIGHT RED

Tzatziki

Recipes for this are legion: some have mint; some do not call for garlic.

SERVES 6
1 medium cucumber
570ml/1 pint low-fat plain yoghurt
1 garlic clove, crushed
freshly ground black pepper

1. Cut the cucumber into very fine dice. Place in a sieve, sprinkle liberally with salt and leave to 'degorge' for 30 minutes. Rinse very well, drain and pat dry.

2. Mix the cucumber with the yoghurt, garlic and plenty of black pepper.

NOTE: The yoghurt can be thickened by draining it in a muslin-lined sieve; this will make for a creamier finish.

WHITE ALSACE

Aubergine Loaf

340g/12oz aubergines, peeled and diced
2 garlic cloves, crushed and fried in 15ml/1/2
    tablespoon of olive oil
2 eggs
225ml/8 fl oz Greek yoghurt
pinch of ground cumin
30g/1oz creamed coconut
salt and pepper

1. Set the oven to 150°C/300°F/gas mark 2. Oil a 450g/1lb loaf tin and line with greaseproof paper.

2. Steam the aubergines for about 10 minutes or until softened.

3. Mix together the garlic, eggs, yoghurt, cumin, coconut, salt and pepper. Add the aubergines.

4. Pour into the prepared loaf tin and cover with foil. Place in a bain-marie in the preheated oven for 40 minutes or until firm.

5. Allow to cool and serve cut in slices with a tomato sauce or salad.

MEDIUM RED

Tomato, Mozzarella and Avocado Salad

55g/2oz tomatoes per person, skinned and
  sliced
55g/2oz mozzarella cheese per person, sliced
1/4 avocado pear per person, sliced
fresh basil, finely chopped
French dressing (see page 136)
black olives
salt and freshly ground black pepper

1. Lay the tomato, avocado pear and cheese in overlapping slices.

2. Add the basil to the dressing. Pour over the salad and sprinkle with a few olives. Season well with salt and plenty of freshly ground black pepper.

SOAVE/FRASCATI

Three-pea Salad

SERVES 8
110g/4oz brown lentils
110g/4oz chickpeas, soaked for 3 hours
110g/4oz split green peas
150ml/1/4 pint French dressing (see page 136)
5ml/1 teaspoon chopped fresh mint
15ml/1 tablespoon chopped fresh parsley
5ml/1 teaspoon French mustard
salt

1. Cook the lentils, chickpeas and split green peas in separate pans of boiling water. The lentils and split peas will take anything from 30 to 75 minutes, and the chickpeas up to 2 hours. Rinse them all under cold water and drain well.

2. Shake the dressing in a jar until well emulsified and divide equally between three cups. To one cup add the mint; to another, the parsley; and to the third, the mustard. Add a good pinch of salt to each. Toss the chickpeas in the parsley vinaigrette, the split peas in the minty dressing and the lentils in the mustard one.

3. Arrange the piles of dressed peas on a serving dish or hors d'oeuvres tray.

NOTE: Other pulses, such as soya beans, red kidney beans and haricot beans are good treated similarly.

ALSACE WHITE

Melon, Cucumber and Tomato Salad

6 tomatoes, peeled, deseeded and slivered
1 cucumber, cubed
1 medium-sized ripe melon, deseeded and cut
    into balls
French dressing (see page 136)
15ml/1 tablespoon chopped mint

1. Mix all the ingredients together with the French dressing and chopped mint. Serve well chilled.

DRY WHITE

Grilled Pepper Salad

SERVES 4
6 large peppers – 2 red, 2 yellow, 2 green
3 hardboiled eggs
30ml/2 tablespoons extra virgin olive oil
freshly ground black pepper

1. Cut the peppers into quarters and remove the stalks, inner membranes and seeds. Heat the grill to its highest temperature.

2. Grill the peppers, skin side uppermost, until the skin is black and blistered. With a small knife, scrape off all the skin.

3. Cut the flesh into shapes like petals, and arrange them like a flower on a flat round dish, garnishing with the hardboiled eggs, cut into quarters. Pour over the olive oil and sprinkle with a little black pepper.

ALSACE WHITE

Vegetable Pasta

SERVES 4
4 medium courgettes
4 carrots
French dressing (see page 136)
15ml/1 tablespoon finely chopped chives

1. Peel the carrots, then continue using the potato peeler, and shred the carrots into long thin ribbons.

2. Top and tail the courgettes, then proceed as for the carrots, and shred the courgettes into long thin ribbons.

3. Toss the carrots and courgettes in the French dressing at least 2 hours before serving so that the vegetables begin to curl.

4. Arrange on individual plates garnished with the chives.

ALSACE WHITE

Tabouleh

Recipes for this are legion. The important thing is that it should be green and have a good lemon flavour.

SERVES 4
110g/4oz cracked wheat
1 tomato, peeled, deseeded and chopped
1/2 cucumber, chopped
10 leaves fresh mint, finely chopped
good handful of fresh parsley, finely chopped
1 shallot, finely chopped
45ml/3 tablespoons olive oil
salt and freshly ground black pepper
lemon juice

1. Soak the wheat in cold water for 15 minutes – it will expand greatly. Drain and wrap in a clean tea towel. Squeeze out the moisture. Spread the wheat on a tray to dry further.

2. Mix all the ingredients together, adding salt, pepper and plenty of lemon juice to taste.

DRY WHITE

Crudités

A selection of:
celery
green pepper
cauliflower
radishes
button mushrooms
spring onions
carrots
asparagus
cherry tomatoes
tiny mangetout
baby sweetcorns
young turnips
black olives

For the dressing:
1 garlic clove, crushed (optional)
150ml/¼ pint mayonnaise (see page 141)

1. Prepare the vegetables, making sure they are perfectly clean, and as far as possible evenly sized.
Celery: wash and cut into sticks.
Pepper: wipe and cut into strips, discarding the seeds.
Cauliflower: wash and break into florets. Peel the stalks if tough.
Radishes: wash and trim off the root and long leaves, but leave a little of the green stalk.
Mushrooms: wash. Peel only if the skins are tough. Quarter if large.
Spring onions: wash. Cut off most of the green part, and the beard (roots). Leave whole, or cut in half lengthways if large.
Carrots: peel and cut into sticks the same shape and size as the celery.
Asparagus: peel the tough outer stalk and trim away the hard root ends.
Turnip: peel and cut into strips. (Use young turnips only.)
Black olives: stone with a cherry stoner if desired.

2. Mix the garlic (if using) with the mayonnaise. Then spoon it into a small serving bowl.

3. Arrange the raw prepared vegetables and the olives in neat clumps on a tray or flat platter with the bowl of mayonnaise dip in the centre.

NOTE: These crudités can also be served with any of the dips on page 147.

LIGHT RED

Marinated Italian Aubergines and Courgettes

This recipe has been adapted from a similar recipe by Sophie Grigson.

SERVES 8
450g/1lb small courgettes (yellow or green)
450g/1lb small aubergines
salt and freshly ground black pepper
olive oil
1 large onion, roughly chopped
1 carrot, diced
5 sage leaves, roughly torn
juice of 1 lemon
60ml/4 tablespoons white wine
240ml/8 fl oz white wine vinegar
3 juniper berries
1 bay leaf
2 sprigs parsley

1. Trim the ends off the courgettes and aubergines and cut into quarters lengthways.

2. Place in a colander, sprinkle with salt and leave to degorge for 30 minutes.

3. Rinse and dry the vegetables and fry in olive oil until lightly browned and just tender. The aubergines will take considerably longer to cook than the courgettes. Transfer, skin side up, to an ovenproof dish.

4. Meanwhile, put the remaining ingredients into a large saucepan. Bring them up to the boil and simmer for 2 minutes.

5. When all the courgettes and aubergines are cooked, reheat the vinegar marinade and pour it over the vegetables. Leave to cool. Cover and refrigerate for 2 days.

6. Remove and discard any bedraggled herbs and vegetables. Bring back to room temperature before serving.

SOAVE/FRASCATI

Cucumber with Soured Cream

1 medium cucumber

For the dressing:
45ml/3 tablespoons oil
15ml/1 tablespoon wine vinegar
salt and pepper
pinch of sugar
15ml/1 level tablespoon chopped mint

For the topping:
55g/2oz soft cream cheese
30ml/2 tablespoons soured cream
1 small garlic clove, crushed
juice of 1/2 lemon

1. Slice the cucumber finely. Sprinkle the slices lightly with salt and leave for 20 minutes.

2. Put the dressing ingredients in a screw-top jar and shake until well emulsified.

3. Beat the cream cheese until soft, then gradually stir in the soured cream. Add the garlic, and season with salt, pepper and lemon juice to taste.

4. Rinse, drain and dry the cucumber thoroughly. Toss the slices in the French dressing and put them into a serving dish, or on to individual plates. Spoon the cream cheese mixture on top.

NOTE: This makes a good salad, with others, for a party, or can be served with hot bread and butter as a light first course.

MEDIUM DRY WHITE

Aubergines Robert

SERVES 4
2 aubergines
150ml/1/4 pint French dressing (see page 136)
5ml/1 teaspoon chopped fresh chives

1. Slice the aubergines and soak them in the dressing for 2 hours.

2. Heat the grill.

3. Grill the aubergines on both sides until pale brown. Sprinkle well with chives and more dressing and grill again for 1 minute or until golden brown. Turn the slices over, sprinkle again with dressing and chives, and grill to a good brown.

4. Allow to cool. Chill well before serving.

ROSE

Vegetable Surprises

SERVES 4

2 large carrots, peeled and sliced thinly
  lengthways
1 small mouli, peeled and sliced thinly
  lengthways
2 large courgettes, sliced thinly lengthways
8 leaves spinach, stems removed
225g/8oz silken tofu
15ml/1 tablespoon light soy sauce
2 small beetroot, peeled and cut into
  julienne strips
8 basil leaves
8 spring onions, cut into 5cm/2 inch
  julienne strips

For the sauce:
400g/14oz natural yoghurt
1 garlic clove, crushed
15ml/1 tablespoon chopped fresh coriander
30ml/2 tablespoons Indonesian soy sauce
  (kecap manis) or light soy sauce
ground cumin
salt and freshly ground black pepper

To garnish:
mustard cress

1. Blanch and refresh the carrots, mouli and courgette slices. Drain well and dry on absorbent paper.

2. Cut the spinach leaves into 8 x 5cm/2 inch squares. Refresh, drain and dry on absorbent paper.

3. Mix together the tofu and light soy sauce.

4. Lay the spinach leaves out on the work top. Cover with the julienne of beetroot, the basil leaves, spring onions and a dollop of tofu and soy sauce. Roll up to form a cylinder.

5. Roll each cylinder first in a courgette slice, then in a mouli slice and finally in a carrot slice. The julienne of vegetables should sprout out of the roll of sliced vegetables.

6. Wrap the rolls tightly in cling wrap and leave to stand in the refrigerator for at least 1 hour.

7. Mix together the yoghurt, garlic, coriander and soy sauce. Season to taste with the cumin, salt and pepper. Chill before serving.

8. Unwrap the vegetable surprises and arrange on a plate. Place a dollop of sauce on each plate and garnish with the mustard cress.

DRY WHITE

Niçoise Vegetables

SERVES 4-6

1 bay leaf
sprig of thyme
1/2 cauliflower, broken into florets
110g/4oz French beans, topped, tailed and
*   halved*
110g/4oz carrots, cut into julienne
2 large courgettes, cut into julienne
about 8 button mushrooms, trimmed
about 8 button onions, peeled
2 tomatoes, skinned and quartered

For the vinaigrette dressing:
90ml/6 tablespoons olive oil
30ml/2 tablespoons wine vinegar
2.5ml/1/2 teaspoon salt
2.5ml/1/2 teaspoon freshly ground black pepper
15ml/1 tablespoon fresh mixed chopped herbs
*   (parsley, mint, tarragon, chives)*
1 garlic clove, crushed

1. Combine the dressing ingredients in a
screw-top jar and shake well.

2. Place a pan of salted water on to boil,
adding the bay leaf and thyme. In it, one
variety at a time, cook all the vegetables
except the tomatoes until just 'al dente'.

3. As soon as they are cooked, lift them out
of the water with a perforated spoon and
dunk them in a bowl of cold water to stop
further cooking and set the colour.

4. Drain the vegetables very well, toss
them in the vinaigrette, and put them and
the tomatoes on a serving dish. Chill
before serving.

NOTE: Peeling onions after boiling is
easier than before, but the boiling water
should not be used to cook the other
vegetables – it will be murky brown.

DRY WHITE

Grilled Aubergines with Pesto

SERVES 4
2 medium aubergines, sliced
salt
150ml/¹/₄ pint French dressing (see page 136)
parsley pesto sauce (see page 145-6)
10ml/2 teaspoons French mustard

1. Sprinkle the aubergine slices liberally with salt and leave for 30 minutes.

2. Make the French dressing and season with the mustard.

3. Rinse the aubergines, drain and dry well. Soak them in the French dressing for 2 hours. Drain well.

4. Heat the grill.

5. Grill the aubergines for about 10 minutes on each side, or until soft and pale brown.

6. Spread one side of the aubergine with the pesto sauce and return to the grill for 1 minute.

7. Arrange on a round plate.

LIGHT RED/ROSE

Mushrooms à la Grecque

SERVES 4
425ml/³/₄ pint water
30ml/2 tablespoons tomato purée
30ml/2 tablespoons olive oil
30ml/2 tablespoons white wine
2 shallots, finely chopped
1 garlic clove, crushed
6 coriander seeds
2.5ml/¹/₂ teaspoon dried or 5ml/1 teaspoon
  chopped fresh fennel
6 peppercorns
small pinch of salt
pinch of sugar
good squeeze of lemon juice
450g/1lb button mushrooms, wiped and
  trimmed
10ml/2 teaspoons chopped parsley

1. Place all the ingredients except the mushrooms and parsley in a saucepan and simmer gently for 15-20 minutes.

2. Add the mushrooms and simmer for 10 minutes. Remove the mushrooms. Taste.

3. Unless it tastes very strong, reduce the liquid by boiling to about 190ml/¹/₃ pint. Put the mushrooms back and allow to cool.

4. Check the seasoning and tip into a shallow bowl or dish. Sprinkle with chopped parsley.

BEAUJOLAIS

Mushroom Roulade

SERVES 4-6

450g/1lb mature black cap mushrooms
30g/1oz butter
30g/1oz flour
1 teaspoon tomato purée
1 teaspoon mushroom ketchup (optional)
pinch of freshly grated nutmeg
salt and freshly ground black pepper
4 eggs, separated

For the filling:
225g/8oz cream cheese
*60ml/4 tablespoons fromage frais or natural
   yoghurt*
4 medium spring onions, finely sliced
*15ml/1 tablespoon chopped herbs (e.g. parsley,
   thyme, sage, chervil)*
salt and freshly ground black pepper

1. Preheat the oven to 200°C/400°F/gas mark 6. Place the mushrooms in a food processor with 15ml/1 tablespoon water. Process until very finely chopped.

2. Melt the butter in a large saucepan, add the flour and cook together for half a minute.

3. Add the chopped mushrooms and stir well. Heat steadily and cook, stirring occasionally, until the mushrooms are fairly dry. (They will, at first, throw out a lot of liquid which needs to be evaporated.) This may take up to 20 minutes. Meanwhile, line a large roasting tin with a double sheet of greased greaseproof paper or silicone paper, letting the edges stick up over the sides of the tin.

4. Remove from the heat and add the tomato purée, mushroom ketchup, nutmeg, and salt and pepper to taste. Stir in the egg yolks and turn into a large bowl.

5. In another large bowl whip the egg whites with a balloon whisk until they will hold their shape. Take a spoonful of egg white and add to the mushroom mixture, stirring it in to loosen the mixture.

6. Fold the remaining egg whites into the mixture and carefully spread the mixture into the prepared roasting tin, taking care not to lose any air.

7. Place in the preheated oven for approximately 12 minutes, or until the roulade is firm to the touch.

8. Meanwhile, prepare the filling. With a wooden spoon, let down the cream cheese carefully with the fromage frais, stirring well to ensure no lumps are left. Add the spring onions, herbs, salt and pepper.

9. When the roulade is cooked, turn it on to a piece of greaseproof paper, trim the edges, spread over the filling and roll it up carefully, letting it rest on the seam. Wrap tightly with the greaseproof paper and place in the refrigerator for about half an hour or until cold.

LIGHT RED

Spinach Roulade

SERVES 4

450g/1lb fresh spinach, or 170g/6oz frozen leaf
*   spinach, cooked and chopped*
4 eggs, separated
15g/¹/₂oz butter
salt and freshly ground black pepper
pinch of nutmeg

For the filling:
15g/¹/₂oz butter
170g/6oz mushrooms, chopped
15g/¹/₂oz flour
150ml/¹/₄ pint milk
60ml/4 tablespoons cream
15ml/1 tablespoon chopped fresh parsley
salt and freshly ground black pepper

1. Line a roasting tin with a double layer of lightly greased greaseproof paper. Allow the edges to stick above the sides of the tin.

2. Melt the butter for the filling and gently cook the mushrooms in it. Remove the pan from the heat, add the flour and mix well. Return the pan to the heat and cook for half a minute. Add the milk and bring to the boil, stirring continually until you have a fairly thick creamy sauce. Add the cream and parsley and season to taste. Beat in the butter.

3. Set the oven to 190°C/375°F/gas mark 5.

4. To make the roulade, gradually beat the egg yolks and butter into the spinach and season with salt, pepper and nutmeg. Whisk the egg whites until stiff but not dry and fold them into the spinach. Pour this

mixture into the prepared roasting tin, spread it flat. Bake for 10-12 minutes or until it feels dry to the touch.

5. Put a piece of greaseproof paper on top of a tea towel. Turn the roulade out on to the paper and remove the original piece of paper. Spread the filling on to the roulade and roll it up as you would a Swiss roll, removing the paper as you go. Serve whole on a warmed dish.

LIGHT RED

Spinach and Ricotta Strudels

These strudels can easily be made with bought filo pastry.

SERVES 6

450g/1lb fresh spinach, cooked and chopped
170g/6oz ricotta cheese
1 egg, lightly beaten
salt and black pepper
grated nutmeg
340g/12oz filo or strudel pastry
melted butter

1. Set the oven to 200°C/400°F/gas mark 6.

2. Mix the spinach with the ricotta cheese, and add egg, salt, pepper, and nutmeg to taste.

3. Cut the strudel leaves to 13cm/5 inch squares. Brush each square immediately with melted butter. Lay 2 or 3 squares on top of each other.

4. Put a spoonful of the spinach mixture on each piece of pastry. Fold the sides of the pastry over slightly to prevent the filling escaping during cooking, then roll the strudels up rather like a Swiss roll.

5. Brush with more melted butter and bake in the prepared oven on a greased baking sheet for 15 minutes.

NOTE: An alternative method of preparing the pastry is to cut up the strudel into long strips, then place a spoonful of the filling in the top right-hand corner and fold it up into successive triangles as shown in the illustration below.

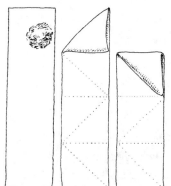

Put a spoonful of filling in the top right-hand corner and fold the pastry into successive triangles

SPICY DRY WHITE/LIGHT RED

Spinach Moulds

SERVES 6
30g/1oz butter
675g/1¹/₂lb spinach leaves, destalked
  and washed
225g/8oz ricotta cheese
30g/1oz Gruyère, grated
30g/1oz Parmesan, grated
2 eggs
60ml/4 tablespoons single cream
grated nutmeg
salt and freshly ground black pepper

1. Lightly butter 6 ramekin dishes.

2. Blanch 10 spinach leaves, refresh, drain and dry well.

3. Arrange the leaves inside the ramekin dishes, overlapping the edges.

4. Cook the remaining leaves for 2 minutes, drain very well by squeezing between 2 plates. Chop finely. Set the oven to 200°C/400°F/gas mark 6.

5. Mix together the cheeses, eggs, cream and seasoning.

6. Fill the ramekin dishes with alternate layers of the cheese mixture and the spinach. Fold over the spinach leaves.

7. Dot butter on each ramekin. Set in a bain-marie and bake for 25-30 minutes. Rest for 2 minutes before unmoulding.

SPICY DRY WHITE/LIGHT RED

Celeriac Rémoulade

SERVES 4
450g/1lb celeriac
45ml/3 tablespoons mayonnaise (see page 141)
2.5ml/¹/₂ teaspoon Dijon mustard
10ml/2 teaspoons finely chopped gherkin
10ml/2 teaspoons finely chopped fresh tarragon
  or chervil
10ml/2 teaspoons finely chopped capers

1. Mix together all the ingredients except the celeriac.

2. Peel the celeriac and cut into very fine matchsticks. Blanch briefly in boiling water, refresh and drain well. Mix with the sauce, before it has time to discolour.

3. Turn into a clean dish.

NOTE: Rémoulade sauce is a mayonnaise with a predominantly mustard flavour. The other ingredients, though good, are not always present.

SPICY DRY WHITE

Sweet Potato and Spinach Pots

SERVES 6
900g/2lb sweet potatoes
salt and freshly ground black pepper
45g/1½ oz butter, plus a little extra for
*   spreading*
2 egg yolks
170g/6oz fresh spinach (choose as large leaves
*   as possible)*

To garnish:
225g/8oz cherry tomatoes, halved

1. Wash and peel the potatoes and cook in lightly salted boiling water until tender, about 20-30 minutes. Drain well.

2. Mash the potatoes and add the butter, egg yolks, salt and pepper. Mash until smooth.

3. Preheat the oven to 180°C/350°F/gas mark 4.

4. Lightly butter 6 ramekin dishes.

5. Wash the spinach, remove any tough stalks and blanch in boiling water until just tender. Refresh thoroughly and drain well.

6. Line the ramekin dishes with the spinach leaves. Spoon the sweet potato mixture into the centre and fold the spinach leaves over the mixture to cover.

7. Place the ramekins in a roasting tin and pour boiling water into this to a depth of

1cm/½ inch. Then bake for 30-40 minutes or until the potato mixture is heated right through and set.

8. Invert on a warm plate, garnish with the cherry tomatoes and serve.

MEDIUM DRY WHITE

Spinach Timbale

SERVES 4-6

675g/1½lb fresh spinach
30g/1oz butter
85g/3oz fresh white breadcrumbs, sieved
2 eggs, beaten
1 egg yolk
pinch of ground nutmeg
salt and freshly ground black pepper
345ml/12 fl oz milk

To serve:
tomato dressing (see page 136)

1. Wash the spinach well and remove the tough stalks. Blanch, refresh and drain 15 of the biggest and best leaves. Put the rest of the still wet spinach into a saucepan with a lid and, holding the pan in one hand and the lid on with the other, shake and toss the spinach over heat until it is soft and reduced in quantity.

2. Squeeze all the water from the spinach, pressing it between 2 plates. Tip on to a board and chop very finely. Butter a 15cm/6 inch cake tin or soufflé dish and line it with the whole spinach leaves.

3. In a saucepan melt the butter, add the spinach and stir until very dry looking. Take off the heat and add the breadcrumbs, eggs, egg yolk, nutmeg and seasoning.

4. Heat the milk and then stir it into the mixture.

5. Spoon the spinach mixture into the cake tin and cover with buttered foil or greaseproof paper. Then heat the oven to 180°C/350°F/gas mark 4. Stand the cake tin in a roasting pan full of boiling water. Transfer both roasting tin and spinach mould to the oven and bake for 45 minutes or until the mixture is firm.

6. Turn out on a hot serving dish.

NOTE: Individual spinach timbales can be made in ramekin dishes. They will take 20-30 minutes to cook. The finer the china, the more quickly the mixture will cook.

SPICY DRY WHITE

Carrot and Spinach Timbales

SERVES 6
340g/12oz carrots, peeled and sliced
2 eggs, beaten
290ml/¹/₂ pint double cream
salt and freshly ground black pepper
pinch of cumin
340g/12oz spinach, tough stalks removed
pinch of nutmeg

1. Cook the carrots in boiling salted water until very tender. Drain well, whizz in a food processor and push through a sieve. Cool, then stir in half the beaten egg, and half the double cream, and season with cumin, salt and pepper.

2. Cook the spinach in a very little boiling water until tender. Drain very well, cool slightly and whizz in a food processor with the remaining beaten egg and cream. Season with grated nutmeg, salt and pepper.

3. Line the bottom of 6 timbale moulds or ramekins with circles of greased greaseproof paper. Spoon in the thicker of the two purées, and carefully pile on the other purée.

4. Preheat the oven to 180°C/350°F/gas mark 4. Cook the timbales in a bain-marie for about 40 minutes or until set. Turn out to serve.

NOTE: If spinach is not available, broccoli can be used in its place.

MEDIUM DRY WHITE

Carrot and Gruyère Timbales

SERVES 4
170g/6oz grated carrot
85g/3oz grated Gruyère cheese
1 egg, beaten
salt and freshly ground black pepper
2.5ml/¹/₂ teaspoon dry English mustard
30ml/2 tablespoons double cream
butter

To serve:
tomato sauce (see page 139)

1. Set the oven to 190°C/375°F/gas mark 5.

2. Blanch the carrot in boiling water for 30 seconds. Refresh under cold running water and drain well on absorbent paper. Mix together the carrot, cheese, egg, salt, pepper, mustard and cream. Beat well.

3. Butter 4 dariole moulds and pour in the carrot and cheese mixture. Cover with lids and put the moulds into a roasting tin half filled with very hot water.

4. Bake for 20 minutes. Carefully turn each mould out on a serving dish or plate. Hand the tomato sauce separately.

LIGHT RED

Courgette and Carrot Roulade

SERVES 6
110g/4oz carrots
110g/4oz courgettes
4 eggs, separated

For the filling:
110g/4oz cream cheese
30ml/2 tablespoons yoghurt
4 spring onions, finely sliced
1 tablespoon finely chopped mixed herbs,
  e.g. parsley, thyme
grated rind of 1/2 lemon
salt and freshly ground black pepper

1. Put a double layer of lightly oiled greaseproof paper into a large roasting tin. Set the oven to 190°C/375°F/gas mark 5.

2. Grate the carrots and courgettes, mix them together with the egg yolks and season well with salt and pepper. Whisk the egg whites to medium peaks and fold them carefully into the carrots and courgettes.

3. Pour this mixture into the lined roasting tin, spread it flat. Bake for 10-12 minutes or until it feels dry to the touch.

4. Meanwhile, mix together the ingredients for the filling. Season to taste.

5. When the roulade is cooked, turn it out on to a clean sheet of greaseproof paper. Trim the edges, spread with the filling and roll up carefully. Serve cold.

DRY WHITE

Courgette Timbales

SERVES 6
450g/1lb courgettes
salt and freshly ground black pepper
2 eggs
1 egg yolk
55g/2oz fresh white breadcrumbs, sieved
290ml/1/2 pint milk
15ml/1 tablespoon fresh thyme, chopped

1. Set the oven to 170°C/325°F/gas mark 3.

2. Oil and line 6 ramekin dishes with a disc of lightly oiled greaseproof paper.

3. Top, tail and grate the courgettes. Sprinkle sparingly with salt. Leave in a sieve for half an hour. Rinse and dry well on kitchen paper.

4. Lightly beat the eggs and egg yolk together. Add the breadcrumbs, milk, thyme and courgettes. Season well with salt and pepper.

5. Pour into the prepared ramekin dishes. Cover with lightly oiled greaseproof paper and place in a hot bain-marie. Put in the centre of the preheated oven for 40 minutes or until the timbales are set.

6. Serve warm.

DRY WHITE

Cucumber Mousse

SERVES 4

1 large cucumber, peeled if preferred
110g/4oz full fat cream cheese
150ml/¹/₄ pint double cream, whipped or
*   yoghurt or soured cream*
salt and freshly ground black pepper
pinch of grated nutmeg
juice of 1 lemon
10ml/2 teaspoons of agar-agar (see NOTE I*)*
150ml/¹/₄ pint vegetable stock

1. Grate the cucumber, reserving about 2.5cm/1 inch to slice for decoration. Put the grated cucumber into a sieve. Leave to drain for 15 minutes.

2. Oil a soufflé dish or mould, and stand upside down to drain off excess.

3. Beat together the cream cheese and whipped cream, yoghurt or soured cream. Mix in the grated cucumber and season with salt, pepper and nutmeg. Add the lemon juice.

4. In a small pan, soak the agar-agar in the stock for 5 minutes. Warm over a very gentle heat until runny (this may take 20 minutes.) Boil for 1 minute and add to the cucumber mixture, mixing gently but thoroughly. Pour into the prepared mould and chill in the refrigerator.

5. To turn out, invert a plate over the mould and turn plate and mould over together. Give a sharp shake to dislodge the mousse. Then decorate with slices of cucumber.

NOTE I: The easiest and most readily available agar-agar comes in powdered form. The basic rule is that 1 teaspoon of agar-agar will set 290ml/¹/₂pint of liquid ingredients or 280/10oz weighed ingredients.

The agar-agar should be soaked for about 5 minutes (about a teaspoon to 150ml/¹/₄ pint) and then dissolved over a low heat until completely runny. This may take 20 minutes. It should then be boiled for 1 minute. If it begins to become gluey add a little extra water. The mixture must be liquid when it is used. If you want to make sure that it will set, spoon a tiny bit on to a cold plate – a skin should form very quickly and will wrinkle if a finger is pulled over it. Agar-agar has to be treated carefully – do not stir it while it is melting and do not beat it into your other ingredients – it will lose some of its setting powers. All ingredients used should be at room temperature. Agar-agar may set your ingredients before the mixture is cool. Recipes that have a high acidity and low sugar content should be made and eaten on the same day – there is a tendency for these dishes to secrete liquid if kept overnight.

NOTE II: If a velvety texture is required, blend the cucumber with the yoghurt or cream in a liquidizer.

NOTE III: This mousse does not keep well. Eat within 24 hours.

DRY WHITE

Red Pepper Bavarois with Red Pepper Salad

SERVES 8

3 red peppers, quartered and deseeded
3 small garlic cloves, finely chopped
1 onion, finely sliced
15ml/1 tablespoon olive oil
salt and freshly ground black pepper
4 large egg yolks
290ml/½ pint milk
15ml/3 teaspoons of agar-agar (see NOTE I,
*   page 36)*
150ml/¼ pint double cream
150ml/¼ pint natural low-fat yoghurt
5ml/1 teaspoon chilli sauce

To serve:
red pepper salad (see page 79)

1. Preheat the grill to its highest setting. Grill the peppers, skin side up, until they are blistered and blackened all over. Place under cold running water and remove the skins. Cut the peppers into strips.

2. Cook the peppers, garlic and onion gently in the olive oil until soft but not brown. Allow to cool and then purée in a food processor and push through a sieve. Season with salt and pepper.

3. Beat the egg yolks. Put the milk into a saucepan and heat until scalding. Pour on to the egg yolks stirring all the time. Return the mixture to the saucepan and heat gently until the custard coats the back of a wooden spoon. Do not allow it to boil. Strain into the purée.

4. Whip the cream lightly and mix it with the yoghurt and the chilli sauce.

5. Fold the cream mixture into the custard

6. Put 150ml/¼ pint of water into a saucepan, sprinkle on the agar-agar and leave it for 5 minutes. Lightly oil a charlotte mould or 20cm/9 inch cake tin. Heat the agar-agar gently until clear and dissolved, this may take 20 minutes. Boil for 2 minutes. Add it to the custard and cream. Pour into the prepared mould. Refrigerate until set.

7. Dip the mould quickly into very hot water and turn out on to a plate. Serve with the red pepper salad.

MEDIUM DRY WHITE

Cheese Soufflé

SERVES 2

40g/1¼ oz butter
dry white breadcrumbs
30g/1oz flour
2.5ml/½ teaspoon made English mustard
pinch of cayenne pepper
290ml/½ pint milk
85g/3oz strong Cheddar or Gruyère
  cheese, grated
4 eggs, separated
salt and pepper

1. Set the oven to 200°C/400°F/gas mark 6. Melt a knob of the butter and brush out a 15cm/6 inch soufflé dish with it. Dust lightly with the breadcrumbs.

2. Melt the rest of the butter in a saucepan and stir in the flour, mustard and cayenne pepper. Cook for 45 seconds. Add the milk and cook, stirring vigorously, for 2 minutes. The mixture will get very thick and leave the sides of the pan. Take it off the heat.

3. Stir in the cheese, egg yolks, salt and pepper. Taste; the mixture should be very well seasoned.

4. Whisk the egg whites until stiff, but not dry, and mix a spoonful into the mixture. Then fold in the rest and pour into the soufflé dish, which should be about two-thirds full. Run your finger around the top of the soufflé mixture. This gives a 'top hat' appearance to the cooked soufflé.

5. Bake for 25-30 minutes and serve straight away. (Do not test to see if the soufflé is done for a least 20 minutes. Then open the oven just wide enough to get your hand in and give the soufflé a slight shove. If it wobbles alarmingly, cook a further 5 minutes.)

SPICY DRY WHITE

Courgette Soufflé

SERVES 4

melted butter
625g/1lb 6oz small dark green courgettes
salt
55g/2oz unsalted butter
45g/1½oz flour
150ml/¼ pint milk infused with a
*   slice of onion*
30g/1oz fresh Parmesan cheese, grated
30g/1oz Cheddar cheese, grated
2 egg yolks
4 egg whites

1. Preheat the oven to 180°C/350°F/gas mark 4 and brush 6 ramekin dishes with butter.

2. Trim the courgettes. Slice 450g/1lb of them very finely. Place in a colander or sieve and sprinkle with 25ml/1½ teaspoons of salt. Mix in well and allow to drain for at least an hour.

3. Cut the remaining courgettes into 6mm/¼inch dice. Salt and drain.

4. Rinse the sliced courgettes and put in a pan with 150ml/¼pint water. Bring to the boil and cook for 5 minutes. Liquidize until smooth.

5. Melt 45g/1½oz butter in a medium-sized saucepan, add the flour and cook over a gentle heat for about 3 minutes, stirring occasionally. Cool slightly.

6. Gradually add the flavoured milk and courgette purée to the flour and butter.

Bring up to the boil and cook gently for about 15 minutes, stirring occasionally. Add more water to the sauce if it gets too thick. Remove from the heat.

7. Add the grated cheeses, stir well, allow to cool slightly and then beat in the egg yolks.

8. Melt the remaining butter in a small pan and cook the rinsed, drained and diced courgettes until slightly brown and crisp.

9. Season the sauce and whisk the egg whites until medium peaks are formed. Fold them carefully into the courgette sauce.

10. Half fill each ramekin with the soufflé mixture. Divide the diced courgettes between the ramekins and cover with the remaining mixture.

11. Place the ramekins in a roasting tin half filled with boiling water and put into the top of the oven.

12. Bake for 25-30 minutes until well risen and brown on the top. Serve immediately.

SPICY DRY WHITE

Twice-baked Cheese Soufflés

These little soufflés are wonderfully rich. They can be cooked a few hours before dinner and then re-baked at the last minute.

SERVES 6
290ml/¹/₂ pint milk
slice of onion
pinch of nutmeg
45g/1¹/₂oz butter
45g/1¹/₂oz flour
pinch of dry English mustard
110g/4oz strong Cheddar, grated
3 eggs, separated
salt and pepper
190ml/¹/₃ pint single cream

1. Preheat the oven to 180°C/350°F/gas mark 4. Heat the milk slowly with the onion and nutmeg. Remove the onion.

2. Melt the butter and stir in the flour. Gradually add the milk, off the heat, whisking until smooth.

3. Return to the heat and stir until the sauce boils and thickens. Stop cooking and add the mustard, three-quarters of the cheese and finally the egg yolks. Add salt and pepper.

4. Generously butter 6 teacups or ramekins.

5. Whisk the egg whites until stiff, and fold into the cheese mixture. Spoon into the cups to fill two-thirds full. Stand the cups in a roasting tin of boiling water and bake for 15 minutes or until the mixture is set. Allow to sink and cool.

6. Run a knife round the soufflés to loosen them. Turn them out on to your hand, giving the cups a sharp jerk. Put them, upside down, on a serving dish.

7. Twenty minutes before serving, sprinkle the remaining cheese on top. Season the cream with salt and pepper and pour all over the soufflés, coating them completely. Put the dish into a hot oven, 220°C/425°F/gas mark 7, for 10 minutes or until the soufflé tops are pale gold. Serve fast before they sink.

SPICY DRY WHITE

Cauliflower and Stilton Pudding

SERVES 4

1 medium cauliflower
150ml/¼ pint milk
30g/1oz butter
30g/1oz flour
salt and pepper
nutmeg
55g/2oz Stilton, crumbled
4 eggs
15ml/1 tablespoon grated Cheddar cheese
15ml/1 tablespoon dried breadcrumbs

1. Cut the cauliflower into florets and cook them in a pan of boiling salted water until tender. Drain well and liquidize or sieve to a pulp with the milk.

2. Melt the butter, stir in the flour and cook, stirring, for 1 minute. Pour in the cauliflower purée. Stir until the sauce is boiling and has thickened. Taste and season very well.

3. Butter a 15cm/6 inch soufflé dish and set the oven to 180°C/350°F/gas mark 4.

4. Stir in the Stilton off the heat, returning the pan to the heat only if it does not melt, but being careful not to boil the mixture. Allow to cool slightly.

5. Separate the eggs and beat the yolks into the cauliflower mixture.

6. Whisk the whites until stiff but not dry and fold into the mixture. Pour into the buttered soufflé dish.

7. Sprinkle with cheese and crumbs. Bake in a bain-marie for 20-25 minutes or until well risen, brown on top and fairly steady when given a slight shake. If it wobbles alarmingly, give it another 5 minutes.

MEDIUM DRY WHITE

Gruyère Spoonbread with Vegetables and Butter Sauce

This recipe has been adapted from one cooked at the school by a Mouton Cadet competition entrant.

Spoonbread is a cornmeal-based dish similar to a soufflé but with a denser texture; it is less fragile and temperamental than a soufflé. It is an old American dish based on native American Indian cooking. Other green vegetables can be substituted if broccoli and courgettes are not to hand.

SERVES 6
For the Gruyère spoonbread:
570ml/1 pint milk
150ml/ 1/4 pint double cream
125g/41/2oz fine white or yellow cornmeal
70g/21/2oz butter
5ml/1 teaspoon salt
2.5ml/1/2 teaspoon nutmeg
5ml/1 teaspoon paprika
170g/6oz Gruyère cheese, grated
4 eggs, separated

For the vegetables:
110g/4oz dried flageolet beans
450g/1lb broccoli
1/2 small radicchio lettuce
3 small courgettes, cut into batons
70g/21/2oz chopped walnuts
Butter for sautéing

For the butter sauce:
70g/21/2oz shallots, finely chopped
150ml/1/4 pint wine vinegar or white wine
salt and freshly ground black pepper to taste
285g/10oz butter

For the salad:
1 large head of frisée
juice of 1 lemon
150ml/1/4 pint olive oil

NOTE: Other green vegetables can be used – spinach, asparagus, peas, etc – what's important is that they should be fresh.

1. Boil the dried flageolets for 10 minutes, then simmer for one hour or until tender. Drain and set aside. Boil the broccoli until 'al dente'. Cut into bite-sized pieces.

2. For the spoonbread, bring the milk and cream to the boil and reduce the heat. Gradually add cornmeal, stirring constantly until thick, 3-5 minutes.

3. Remove from the heat and stir in the butter, salt, nutmeg, paprika, cheese and egg yolks. The batter can be prepared in advance up to this point, and stored in the refrigerator until 45 minutes before serving.

4. Whisk the egg whites until stiff but not dry, and fold them into the cornmeal mixture. Pour gently into a well-buttered 1.5 litre/3 pint ring mould, and bake at 175°C/350°F/gas mark 4 for 30-40 minutes. The top should be crusty and the centre soft.

5. Sauté the walnuts in butter for 2 minutes over medium heat. Add the courgettes and sauté for a further minute. Pull off approximately half the leaves of the radicchio and tear into smaller bits. Add to the pan, along with the broccoli and flageolet beans, and sauté until the radicchio leaves turn dark and lose their bitternesss – about 5 minutes.

6. For the butter sauce cook the shallots and vinegar over high heat until reduced by about half. Turn down the heat and add the butter slowly, in little pieces, whisking constantly until creamy, about 10 minutes.

7. Unmould the spoonbread as soon as it comes out of the oven on to a platter, and gently heap the vegetables into the centre and around the edges of the platter. Pour the butter sauce over the vegetables. Serve with the remaining frisée dressed with lemon juice and olive oil.

DRY WHITE

Hummus

This is a spicy hummus and has been adapted from a recipe by one of Leith's most popular guest lecturers, Claudia Roden.

SERVES 4
225g/8oz chickpeas
salt and freshly ground black pepper
10ml/2 teaspoons ground cumin
2 cloves garlic, crushed
juice of 1 lemon
60ml/4 tablespoons olive oil
pinch of cayenne pepper
Greek parsley to garnish

1. Soak the chickpeas overnight in cold water.

2. Drain and cook slowly in clean water for 1-1$^1/_2$ hours. Add the salt towards the end of cooking. Drain and reserve the cooking liquor.

3. Cool for a few minutes and tip into a food processor. Whizz and add the remaining ingredients. Add enough of the cooking liquor to produce a soft cream.

4. Serve on a flat plate garnished with the Greek parsley. Hand hot pitta bread separately.

RETSINA OR DRY WHITE

Stilton and Walnut Pâté

I was given this recipe by Mrs Levis at the Sign of the Angel in Lacock.

SERVES 6
340g/12oz Stilton
450g/1lb Philadelphia cheese
110g/4oz unsalted butter, melted
85g/3oz walnuts
1 glass port
15ml/1 tablespoon chopped chives
salt and freshly ground black pepper

1. Grate or crumble the Stilton cheese. Beat it with the cream cheese. Add the melted butter. Reserve 6 walnuts, chop the rest and add to the pâté.

2. Add the port and chives and season to taste. Pile into a nonstick loaf tin. Cover and refrigerate overnight.

3. Turn out and decorate with the reserved walnuts.

GERMAN WHITE

Guacamole

SERVES 4
2 ripe avocado pears
5ml/1 teaspoon onion juice
juice of 1/2 lemon
10ml/2 teaspoons tomato chutney
10ml/2 teaspoons olive oil
2.5ml/1/2 teaspoon ground coriander
salt and freshly ground black pepper
1 garlic clove, crushed
Tabasco
hot buttered toast

1. Peel the avocado pears and mash them with a fork.

2. Season with the onion juice, lemon juice, tomato chutney, oil, coriander, salt, pepper, garlic and Tabasco.

3. Serve with toast.

SPICY DRY WHITE

Harlequin Omelette

This recipe has been adapted from Roger Vergé's *Cuisine of the Sun*.

SERVES 4-6
75ml/5 tablespoons olive oil
400g/14oz very ripe tomatoes, peeled, deseeded and diced
a pinch of thyme flowers
salt and pepper
500g/1lb 2oz fresh spinach, well washed
2 garlic cloves, peeled
9 eggs
75g/2¹/₂oz Gruyère cheese, grated
120ml/8 tablespoons whipping cream
nutmeg

1. Preheat the oven to 180°C/350°F/gas mark 4.

2. Heat 30ml/2 tablespoons olive oil in a medium-sized saucepan. Add the tomato together with the thyme and a pinch of salt and allow to cook until the moisture from the tomato has evaporated completely.

3. Put 45ml/3 tablespoons olive oil into a larger saucepan and add the spinach, the garlic and a pinch of salt. Stir with a wooden spoon and cook until the moisture has completely evaporated.

4. When the tomatoes and spinach are cooked put them on 2 separate plates, remove the garlic from the spinach, chop finely and allow to cool.

5. Get out 3 bowls and break 3 eggs into each. Add the spinach, 3 tablespoons cream, a grating of nutmeg and salt and pepper to the eggs in the first bowl and whisk everything together. Add the tomatoes, 2 tablespoons cream and salt and pepper to the eggs in the second bowl and whisk. Add the grated Gruyère, 3 tablespoons cream and salt and pepper to the eggs in the third bowl and whisk.

6. Lightly oil the inside of a terrine, and pour in the tomato mixture. Stand the dish in a bain-marie half filled with hot water and cook in the preheated oven for 30 minutes.

7. Very gently, pour in the cheese mixture and return to the oven for a further 10 minutes. Finally pour in the spinach mixture and cook for 20 minutes more.

8. When the omelette is cooked, let it rest for 10-15 minutes in a warm place before turning it out on to a dish. Serve warm, cutting it into slices or wedges according to the shape of the dish it was cooked in.

NOTE I: This omelette can also be served cold, with a little extra virgin olive oil sprinkled on each slice.

NOTE II: Cooking times for each 'omelette' can vary so check that the tomato is just set before adding the cheese and that the cheese is just set before adding the spinach.

DRY WHITE

Terrine de Ratatouille Niçoise

SERVES 10-12

20 large spinach leaves, blanched
    and refreshed
salt and pepper
2 red peppers
2 yellow peppers
2 green peppers
2 aubergines
1 bulb fennel
3 medium courgettes
olive oil

For the mousse:
olive oil
1/2 onion, roughly chopped
2 cloves of new season garlic, crushed
3 red peppers, chopped
2 tomatoes, chopped
2 tablespoons tomato purée
12 basil leaves
a sprig of thyme
15ml/1 tablespoon sugar
150ml/1/4 pint dry white wine
290ml/1/2 pint water
10ml/2 teaspoons of agar-agar (see NOTE I,
    page 36)

For the basil sauce:
25 fresh basil leaves
150ml/1/4 pint mayonnaise (see page 141)
150ml/1/4 pint single cream
lemon juice to taste
salt and pepper

1. Line a 900g/2lb terrine mould first with cling film, then line it with the spinach leaves, overlapping them neatly so that there are no gaps between them. Season lightly.

2. Prepare the vegetables as follows. Peppers: cook in olive oil in the oven at 220°C/425°F/gas mark 7 for 20-25 minutes. Cool, then remove the skins and seeds. Aubergines: cut into 4 lengthways. Cook in olive oil in the oven at 220°C/425°F/ gas mark 7 for 20 minutes. Fennel: peel and separate the layers, and blanch in boiling water for 5-8 minutes. Refresh in iced water and dry. Courgettes: cut into 4 lengthways and shape neatly into pencil thickness. Blanch and refresh, then dry.

3. Prepare the mousse: heat a little oil in a pan, add the onion, garlic, peppers, tomatoes and tomato purée. Season with herbs and sugar, and cook for 4-5 minutes.

4. Add the white wine and cook until reduced by half. Add half of the water and cook gently on the edge of the stove until the vegetables are well cooked, about 15-20 minutes.

5. Purée the mixture in a liquidizer, then pass the purée through a fine sieve. Adjust the seasoning.

6. Soak the agar-agar in the remaining water for 5 minutes. Dissolve over a gentle heat until runny – this may take

20 minutes – boil for 1 minute and add it to the puree.

7. Prepare the terrine: pour 30ml/ 2 tablespoons mousse into the bottom of the spinach-lined mould, cut the yellow peppers to size and cover the terrine from end to end. Season as you go.

8. Pour another 2 tablespoons of mousse on top, then add the aubergine, skin side down first to make a good colour contrast, then another 2 tablespoons of mousse followed by the courgettes. Repeat the process, alternating layers of mousse and vegetable in the following sequence: red pepper, fennel, green pepper, aubergine, yellow pepper. Finish with a layer of mousse.

9. Fold over the spinach leaves carefully to seal the terrine, then cover with cling film. Press the terrine with a weight for 8-24 hours in the refrigerator.

10. Prepare the basil sauce: place all the ingredients in a liquidizer and blend well. Adjust seasoning and consistency.

11. Pour a little sauce on to a plate, cut a slice of terrine and place it on the sauce. Serve chilled.

ROSE/DRY WHITE

Aubergine Caviar

SERVES 8
4 medium aubergines
60ml/4 tablespoons good quality olive oil
4 garlic cloves
30ml/2 tablespoons chopped fresh parsley
salt and freshly ground black pepper
lemon juice to taste

1. Set the oven to 190°C/375°F/gas mark 5.

2. Brush the aubergines with a little oil and bake them until soft (40-60 minutes). After 20 minutes add the whole garlic cloves.

3. Allow the aubergines and garlic to cool.

4. Peel the aubergines, put the flesh into a clean cloth and squeeze dry to extract all the bitter juices.

5. Skin the garlic and put into a food processor with the aubergine flesh, parsley, salt and pepper. Purée until smooth.

6. Gradually beat in the remaining olive oil and when the mixture is stiff stir in the lemon juice and season to taste.

7. Chill in the refrigerator for two hours before serving.

SPICY DRY WHITE OR RETSINA

Spinach Flan

SERVES 2
rich shortcrust pastry made with 110g/4oz
  flour (see page 148)

For the filling:
1/2 onion, finely chopped
15g/1/2oz butter
75ml/5 tablespoons milk
75ml/5 tablespoons single cream
1 egg
1 egg yolk
340g/12oz spinach, cooked and chopped
30g/1oz cheese, strong Cheddar or
  Gruyère, grated
salt and pepper

1. Roll out the pastry and line a flan ring
about 15cm/6 inches in diameter. Leave in
the refrigerator for about 45 minutes to
relax – this prevents shrinkage during
cooking.

2. Set the oven to 200°C/400°F/gas mark 6.

3. Bake the pastry case blind for 10-15
minutes and remove from the oven (see note).

4. Reduce the heat to 150°C/300°F/gas
mark 2.

5. Fry the onion slowly in the butter.
When thoroughly cooked but not
coloured, drain well.

6. Mix together the milk, cream and eggs.
Add the onion, spinach and three-quarters
of the cheese. Season carefully with salt
and pepper (the cheese is salty, so be

careful not to overseason).

7. Pour the mixture into the prepared flan
case and sprinkle over the remaining
cheese. Place the flan in the middle of the
oven and bake for 30-40 minutes.

8. Remove the flan ring to allow the sides
of the pastry to cook evenly and colour.
Bake for a further 5 minutes until the
filling is brown and set.

9. Serve hot or cold.

NOTE: To bake blind, line the raw pastry
case with a piece of foil or a double sheet
of greaseproof paper and fill it with dried
lentils, beans, rice or even pebbles or coins.
This is to prevent the pastry bubbling up
during cooking. When the pastry is half
cooked (about 15 minutes) the 'blind
beans' can be removed and the empty
pastry case further dried out in the oven.
The beans can be re-used indefinitely.

LIGHT RED

Leek en Croute with Mushroom Sauce

SERVES 4

900g/2lb leeks, trimmed and finely sliced
30g/1oz butter
45ml/3 tablespoons double cream
salt and freshly ground black pepper
puff pastry made with 450g/1lb flour (see
*   page 149)*
4 basil leaves
1 egg yolk

To serve:
mushroom sauce (see page 137)

1. Melt the butter in a sauté pan and add the leeks. Cook gently for 1 minute and then add the cream and salt. Cook, stirring occasionally, for approximately 15 minutes or until the leeks have softened and any juices have evaporated. Season with salt and pepper and allow to cool completely.

2. Flour the work surface lightly. Roll the pastry to the thickness of a coin. Using a 10cm/4 inch and a 13cm/5 inch cutter, cut out 4 rounds of each size. If you need to re-roll the pastry, lay the scraps on top of each other and re-roll.

3. Take the 4 smaller circles and divide the leeks between them, leaving a 1cm/1/2inch border clear. Top each mound of leeks with a basil leaf. Dampen the edges lightly with water.

4. Take the larger circles of pastry and carefully place over the filling, ensuring no air is trapped inside. Press the edges lightly together, knock up and crimp the edges.

5. Brush with the egg yolk and then using the back of a sharp knife, mark a criss-cross pattern on the top.

6. Put the leek croustades on a baking sheet and chill in the refrigerator for 30 minutes.

7. Meanwhile, preheat the oven to 200°C/ 400°F/gas mark 6.

8. Bake the leek croustades in the oven for 15-20 minutes or until they are risen and brown.

9. To serve: put 2 leek croustades on each diner's plate and spoon a little sauce around the edge.

DRY WHITE

Spinach and Olive Tart

This recipe has been adapted from Roger Vergé's *Entertaining in the French Style*.

SERVES 6

Provençale pastry made with 340g/12oz flour
   (see page 150)
30ml/2 tablespoons virgin olive oil
2 onions, finely chopped
450g/1lb fresh spinach, cooked and chopped
3 garlic cloves, crushed
3 eggs
45ml/3 tablespoons double cream
salt and pepper
340g/12oz small black Niçoise olives in
   oil, pitted
5ml/1 teaspoon fresh thyme leaves

1. Set the oven to 200°C/400°F/gas mark 6.

2. Heat the oil, add the onions, and cook over a low heat for about 15 minutes until beginning to soften and brown. Add the spinach and garlic and continue to cook over low heat until all the liquid has evaporated. This will take about 8 minutes. Leave to cool.

3. Beat the eggs with the cream. Add the onion and spinach mixture. Mix well and season lightly to taste.

4. Roll out about half of the pastry and use it to line the base of a 30cm/12 inch loose-bottomed flan ring. Bake for 15 minutes.

5. Roll the remaining pastry into strips about 1cm/$\frac{1}{2}$ inch wide and twist into 'ropes'. Put the part-baked flan base back into the flan ring and arrange the 'ropes' of pastry around the edge of the base. Bake for a further 15 minutes.

6. Reduce the heat to 180°C/350°F/gas mark 4.

7. Pour the spinach and onion mixture into the flan case and spread it evenly over the base. Bake for 10 minutes. Remove the flan ring to allow the sides of the pastry to cook and sprinkle the olives evenly over the tart. Dust with the fresh thyme leaves and bake for a further 5 minutes.

8. Serve hot or cold.

PROVENCE ROSE

Leith's Restaurant's Artichoke and Green Olive Pie

SERVES 4

10 fresh globe artichokes
10 shallots, finely diced
2 small garlic cloves, crushed
fresh thyme, chopped
fresh sage, chopped
60ml/4 tablespoons dry white vermouth, or
*   white wine*
860ml/1½ pints double cream
170g/6oz green olives, chopped
salt and freshly ground black pepper
225g/8oz puff pastry (see page 149)
1 egg, beaten

1. Peel the artichokes to the core and then put them immediately into acidulated water.

2. Preheat the oven to 190°C/375°F/gas mark 5.

3. Cut the artichokes into 5mm/¼ inch cubes and cook in the butter very slowly, with the shallots, garlic, thyme and sage, until soft.

4. Add the vermouth or wine. Add the cream and reduce, by boiling, to a coating consistency. Stir the sauce every so often to prevent it from catching on the bottom of the saucepan.

5. Add the olives and season to taste. Leave to cool.

6. Line a 20cm/8 inch flan ring with pastry. Pile in the artichoke and olive mixture and cover the pie with the remaining pastry.

7. Brush with beaten egg and bake for 15-20 minutes or until golden brown.

DRY WHITE

Brioche Stuffed with Wild Mushrooms

SERVES 4
*brioche dough made with 225g/8oz flour
    (see page 156, omitting sugar)*

For the filling:
340g/12oz wild mushrooms, sliced
20g/³/₄oz butter
15ml/1 tablespoon chopped fresh parsley
squeeze of lemon juice
salt and freshly ground black pepper
60ml/4 tablespoons double cream

To glaze:
a little beaten egg

1. Grease a large brioche mould. Roll three-quarters of the dough into a ball and put it into the tin. Make a dip in the centre. Roll the remaining dough into a ball and press into the prepared dip. Press a wooden spoon handle through the smaller of the 2 balls into the brioche base to anchor the top in place while it bakes.

2. Cover with greased polythene and leave in a warm place until risen to the top of the tin. This will take about 30 minutes.

3. Set the oven to 220°C/425°F/gas mark 7.

4. Meanwhile make the filling. Slowly fry the mushrooms in the butter for 1 minute. Then add the parsley, lemon juice, salt and pepper and cream. Taste and set aside.

5. Brush the brioche with beaten egg and bake for 25 minutes. Remove the 'top knot' and some of the inside brioche dough.

6. Heat up the mushroom filling and spoon it into the brioche cavity. It does not matter if it does not all fit in as the final dish looks very attractive if served with some of the filling on the side of the plate. Replace the top and serve immediately.

WHITE ALSACE

Toasted Goats Cheese with Sesame Seeds

SERVES 6
6 small or 3 medium goats cheeses (crotin)
85g/3oz sesame seeds, lightly toasted
6 slices wholemeal toast, cut into circles just
*   larger than the cheese*
2 heads radicchio, washed and dried

For the dressing:
30ml/2 tablespoons olive oil
30ml/2 tablespoons white wine vinegar
1 garlic clove, crushed
30ml/2 tablespoons chopped chives
salt and freshly ground black pepper

1. Preheat the oven to 200°C/400°F/gas mark 6. If you have 3 medium goats cheeses, cut them in half horizontally. Roll the cheeses in the sesame seeds until completely coated.

2. Place the circles of toast on a baking tray and place the cheeses on top. Bake for 5-10 minutes, until the cheese is soft and on the point of melting.

3. Meanwhile, combine all the ingredients for the dressing and mix well. Separate the radicchio into leaves and toss in the dressing. Arrange on 6 plates with the hot toast and cheese on each leaf.

SAUVIGNON BLANC

Goats Cheese with Sesame Seeds in Filo

SERVES 6
6 small or 3 medium goats cheeses (crotin)
85g/3oz sesame seeds, lightly toasted
3 sheets filo pastry
30g/1oz melted butter
2 heads radicchio

For the dressing:
30ml/2 tablespoons olive oil
30ml/2 tablespoons white wine vinegar
1 garlic clove, crushed
30ml/2 tablespoons chopped chives
salt and freshly ground black pepper

1. Preheat the oven to 200°C/400°F/gas mark 6. If you have 3 medium goats cheeses, cut them in half horizontally. Roll the cheese in the sesame seeds until completely coated.

2. Spread out the filo pastry, brush with butter and cut into 12 x 15cm/6 inch squares. Layer one square on top of another. Place a whole or half goats cheese in the centre of each. Draw up the pastry to form 'Dick Whittington' sacks. Lightly dot the outside of the pastry with the melted butter and place on a baking sheet in the hot oven for 5 minutes.

3. Meanwhile, combine all the ingredients for the dressing and mix well. Separate the radicchio into leaves and toss in the dressing. Arrange on 6 plates with the filo parcels.

WHITE LOIRE

Fried Polenta

Polenta is a classical dish of Northern Italy. It can be eaten as soon as it is cooked, or it can be left to cool, sliced and then grilled or fried. This recipe is for fried polenta. It is particularly good served with fried wild mushrooms.

SERVES 4-6
2 litres/3¹/2 pints water
10ml/2 teaspoons salt
285g/10oz coarse cornmeal/maize flour/polenta
oil

1. Put the water and salt into a large saucepan and bring to the boil.

2. Remove from the heat and sprinkle on the cornmeal, whisking quickly to avoid lumps. Reduce the heat.

3. Return the pan to the heat and cover it as the mixture will bubble and spatter.

4. Continue cooking until the polenta is very thick, approximately 35-40 minutes, stirring often to prevent sticking and burning.

5. The polenta can be served at this stage piled high on a plate, or it can be fried as below.

6. Lightly oil a shallow tin 28 cm x 18cm/ 11 x 7 inches. Spread the mixture out evenly, allow to cool, and refrigerate for about 1 hour.

7. Turn the polenta out of the tin, and cut into 4cm/1¹/2 inch slices.

8. Fill a large deep frying pan with enough oil to come 2cm/³/4 inch up the sides of the pan. Heat until very hot.

9. Add the polenta slices, being careful not to overcrowd the pan as this will make turning difficult, reduce the heat and fry gently until golden brown on both sides. Remove with a fish slice, taking care to drain off excess oil.

YOUNG RED

Fried Gnocchi

SERVES 6
570ml/1 pint milk
1 onion, sliced
1 clove
1 bay leaf
6 parsley stalks
110g/4oz semolina
200g/7oz strong Cheddar cheese
30ml/2 tablespoons fresh grated Parmesan
    cheese
15ml/1 tablespoon chopped fresh parsley
salt and freshly ground black pepper
pinch of dried mustard
pinch of cayenne
oil for deep-frying
beaten egg
dried white breadcrumbs

1. Infuse the milk with the onion, clove, bay leaf and parsley stalks over a very gentle heat for 7 minutes. Bring up to boiling point, then strain.

2. Sprinkle in the semolina, stirring steadily, and cook, still stirring, until the mixture is thick (about 1 minute). Draw the pan off the heat and add the cheeses, parsley, salt, pepper, mustard and cayenne. Taste: it should be well seasoned. Then spread this mixture into a neat round on a wet plate and leave to chill for 30 minutes.

3. Cut the gnocchi paste into 8 equal wedges. Chill.

4. Heat the oil until a crumb will sizzle vigorously in it. Dip the gnocchi into beaten egg and coat with breadcrumbs.

5. Deep-fry in hot oil until golden brown (about 2 minutes). Drain well on absorbent paper. Sprinkle with salt and serve.

NOTE I: A thin tomato sauce (see page 139) is good with fried gnocchi.

NOTE II: If you do not like the idea of deep-frying, bake the gnocchi at 190°C/375°F/gas mark 5 for 20 minutes, and then grill until well browned on both sides.

LIGHT RED ITALIAN

Gnocchi alla Romana

SERVES 4-6
1 litre/1³/4 pints milk
7.5ml/1¹/2 teaspoons salt
a good grating of fresh nutmeg
225g/8oz coarse-ground semolina
3 egg yolks
85g/3oz Parmesan cheese, freshly grated
85g/3oz butter

1. Lightly oil an oven tray.

2. In a large saucepan, bring the milk, salt and nutmeg to the boil, remove from the heat and sprinkle over the semolina, stirring it continually with a wooden spoon.

3. Reduce the heat and return the pan to the heat. Continue to cook, uncovered, for 10-15 minutes, stirring occasionally to prevent burning and sticking. The spoon should be able to stand upright, unsupported in the mixture. Remove from the heat. Cool slightly.

4. Beat in the egg yolks, 30g/1oz of the cheese and 30g/1oz of the butter. Taste and season.

5. Pile into the prepared tin and smooth over with a wet spatula to about 5mm/¹/4 inch thick. Refrigerate for about 1-1¹/2 hours until the semolina is firm.

6. Set the oven to 230°C/450°F/gas mark 8. Melt the butter and lightly brush a shallow ovenproof dish with a little of it.

7. Cut the semolina into circles using a 4cm/1¹/2 inch plain pastry cutter. Arrange these discs overlapping each other slightly in the prepared dish.

8. Pour over the remaining butter and sprinkle with the remaining Parmesan cheese. Bake for 15-20 minutes or until crisp and golden brown.

LIGHT RED ITALIAN

Tempura

SERVES 4
For the batter:
225g/8oz flour
2 small egg yolks
340ml/12 fl oz water
pinch of salt

1 small aubergine
1 medium courgette cut into batons
110g/4oz baby sweetcorn, halved lengthways
oil for deep-frying

For the sauce:
10ml/2 teaspoons sesame oil
30ml/2 tablespoons red wine vinegar
30ml/2 tablespoons soy sauce
45ml/3 tablespoons ginger syrup (from a jar of
    preserved ginger)
30ml/2 tablespoons runny honey
1 small bunch spring onions, shredded

1. Slice the aubergine thinly, score the flesh lightly and place in a colander, sprinkling each layer with salt. Leave to 'degorge' for half an hour.

2. Mix all the ingredients together for the sauce, except for the spring onions.

3. Heat the oil for deep-frying until a crumb will sizzle vigorously in it.

4. Wash the aubergines well and pat dry on kitchen paper.

5. When the oil is hot mix the batter ingredients together – it should not be smooth.

6. Dip the prepared ingredients into the batter and deep-fry in small batches. Drain well on kitchen paper and sprinkle lightly with salt. Arrange on a large serving dish.

7. Scatter the shredded spring onions on top of the sauce and hand separately.

SPICY DRY WHITE

Spinach Gnocchi

SERVES 6
170g/6oz fresh spinach, cooked and chopped
225g/8oz ricotta cheese
85g/3oz Parmesan cheese
1 egg
salt and freshly ground black pepper
a good grating of freshly ground nutmeg
flour
45g/1½ oz butter, melted

1. Combine the spinach, ricotta and half the Parmesan cheese in a bowl with the egg, salt, pepper and nutmeg. Mix thoroughly.

2. Place a large pan of salted water on the heat and bring up to simmering point.

3. Meanwhile shape the mixture into egg shapes using a tablespoon and the palm of your hand. Roll the gnocchi lightly in flour. Place them in the simmering water a few at a time and poach gently until they come to the surface, approximately 2-3 minutes.

4. Heat the grill. Remove the gnocchi from the pan with a slotted spoon, allowing excess liquid to drain off. Arrange in an ovenproof dish.

5. Pour over the melted butter, and sprinkle with the remaining Parmesan cheese. Place under the grill for a few minutes until the cheese turns golden brown. Serve immediately.

SOAVE

Onion Tart

SERVES 4
rich shortcrust pastry made with 225g/8oz
*   flour quantity (see page 148)*
55g/2oz butter
15ml/1 tablespoon olive oil
675g/1½lb onions, sliced
2 eggs
2 egg yolks
150ml/¼ pint single cream
salt and pepper
grated nutmeg

1. Preheat the oven to 200°C/400°F/gas mark 6.

2. Roll out the pastry and line a 20cm/8 inch flan ring with it. Leave in the refrigerator to relax for 20 minutes.

3. Melt the butter, add the oil and onions and cook very slowly until soft but not coloured. This may take up to 30 minutes. Leave to cool.

4. Bake the pastry case blind (see note on page 48) then turn the oven down to 175°C/350°F/gas mark 4.

5. Mix together the eggs, cream and onions. Season to taste with salt and pepper. Pour into the pastry case and sprinkle with nutmeg. Bake until golden and just set, about 20 minutes.

BEAUJOLAIS/ALSACE WHITE

Rice and Vegetables

Boiled Rice

55g/2oz long-grain white rice per person
slice of lemon
15ml/1 tablespoon oil

1. Take a large saucepan and fill it with salted water (1 cup of rice will need at least 6 cups of water, but the exact quantities do not matter as long as there is plenty of water). Bring to a rolling boil.

2. Tip in the rice and stir until the water re-boils. Add the lemon slice and oil.

3. Boil for exactly 10 minutes and then test: the rice should be neither hard nor mushy, but firm to the bite: 'al dente'.

4. Drain the rice in a colander or sieve, and swish plenty of hot water through it.

5. Stand the colander on the draining board. With the handle of a wooden spoon, make a few draining holes through the pile of rice to help the water and steam escape. Alternatively, turn the mass of rice over every few minutes with a spoon.

NOTE: If the rice is required for a salad, it may be rinsed in cold water after cooking, but it will need longer to drain dry – if the water is hot it steams dry faster.

Boiled Brown Rice

Brown rices vary enormously, and though this method is suitable for the majority of them, some may require longer, slower cooking.

55g/2oz brown rice per person
salt

1. Cook the rice in a large amount of boiling salted water for 20 minutes. Drain well.

Basmati Rice I

Allow 55g/2oz of rice per head. Soak it in cold water for about 1 hour. Drain, rinse under cold running water, drain well. Put it in a saucepan and add enough cold water to cover, a pinch of salt, a cinnamon stick, 5ml/1 teaspoon lightly fried mustard seeds, and the crushed seeds from 2 or 3 cardamom pods. Bring it to the boil, cover and simmer until the rice is cooked and the water absorbed. This will take 6-9 minutes. Remove the cinnamon stick.

Basmati Rice II

Allow 55g/2oz rice per head. Soak it in cold water for about 1 hour. Drain, rinse well and drain again. Put into a saucepan with a pinch of salt. Add enough cold water to just cover the rice. Bring it up to the boil, simmer for 4-5 minutes, cover and remove from the heat. After about 10 minutes the rice should be perfectly cooked and all the water absorbed.

Brown Rice Pilaf with Sesame Seeds

SERVES 4-6
1 small onion, finely chopped
30g/1oz butter
225g/8oz brown rice
720ml/1¼ pints vegetable stock (see page 136)
45ml/3 tablespoons toasted sesame seeds
15ml/1 tablespoon chopped mixed fresh herbs
salt and freshly ground black pepper
paprika

1. Cook the onion in the butter until it is soft but not coloured.

2. Add the rice and fry, stirring, until it is slightly opaque, about 3 minutes.

3. Add the stock, seeds, herbs, salt and pepper. Bring to the boil, cover and cook very slowly for 45 minutes, by which time the liquid should be completely absorbed and the rice tender.

4. Serve sprinkled with a little paprika.

Mashed Potatoes

SERVES 4
675g/1¹/₂lb potatoes, peeled
about 290ml/¹/₂ pint milk
55g/2oz butter
salt and pepper
a little grated nutmeg

1. Boil the potatoes in salted water until tender. Drain thoroughly.

2. Push the potatoes through a sieve or mouli. Return them to the dry saucepan. Heat carefully, stirring to allow the potato to steam dry.

3. Push the mass of potato to one side of the pan. Put the exposed part of the pan over direct heat and pour in the milk. Tilt the pan to allow the milk to boil without burning the potato.

4. When the milk is boiling, or near it, beat it into the potato. Add the butter. Season with salt, pepper and nutmeg.

NOTE I: This recipe is for very soft mashed potatoes. If you want a stiffer consistency add less milk.

NOTE II: For mashed potatoes with olive oil, add half the quantity of milk, as above, then beat in 150ml/¹/₄ pint olive oil instead of the butter and season to taste.

Potatoes in Coconut Milk

This recipe has been adapted from *Curries and Oriental Cookery* by Josceline Dimbleby.

SERVES 4
55g/2oz unsweetened desiccated coconut
290ml/¹/₂ pint milk
675g/1¹/₂lb potatoes, peeled and cut into chunks
salt
1 small green chilli
2-3 small bay leaves
3 x 2.5cm/1 inch sticks cinnamon

1. Put the coconut in a bowl. Bring the milk to the boil and pour on to the coconut, stir and leave on one side.

2. Boil the potatoes in salted water for 7-10 minutes, until just cooked but not breaking up, and drain.

3. Cut open the chilli under running water, discard the seeds and stem and chop the flesh finely.

4. Return the drained potatoes to a saucepan and strain the coconut milk over them through a fine sieve, pressing to extract all the liquid. Add the bay leaves, the chilli, a little salt and the cinnamon sticks. Bring to the boil and simmer for 8-10 minutes. Transfer to a serving dish.

Roast Potatoes

SERVES 4
900g/2lb potatoes
salt
60ml/4 tablespoons dripping or oil

1. Wash and peel the potatoes and, if they are large, cut them into 5cm/2 inch pieces.

2. Bring them to the boil in salted water. Simmer for 5 minutes.

3. Drain them and shake them in the sieve to roughen and slightly crumble the surface of each potato. (This produces deliciously crunchy potatoes that can be kept warm for up to 2 hours without coming to any harm. Potatoes roasted without this preliminary boiling and scratching tend to become tough and hard if not eaten straight away.)

4. Melt the fat in a roasting pan and add the potatoes, turning them so that they are coated all over.

5. Roast, basting occasionally, turning the potatoes over at half-time. See note below.

NOTE: Potatoes can be roasted at almost any temperature, usually taking 1 hour in a hot oven, or 1¹/2 hours in a medium one. They should be basted and turned over once or twice during cooking, and they are done when a skewer glides easily into them. Potatoes roasted in the same pan as the meat have the best flavour, but this is not always possible if the joint or bird is very large, or if liquid has been added to the pan.

Leith's Good Foods' Dauphinoise Potatoes

900g/2lb old floury potatoes, peeled and finely
*   sliced*
1 onion, finely sliced
1 garlic clove, crushed (optional)
15g/¹/2oz butter
425ml/³/4 pint mixed single and double cream
150ml/¹/4 pint soured cream, let down to
*   double cream consistency with milk*
salt and freshly ground black pepper

1. Preheat the oven to 170°C/325°F/gas mark 3.

2. Cook the onions and garlic in the butter until soft but not brown.

3. Layer up the potatoes and creams with the onions and seasoning in a lightly buttered dish, and bake in the oven for 1¹/2 hours.

Rösti Potatoes

SERVES 4
1 Spanish onion, finely chopped
oil
675g/1¹/2lb large potatoes, peeled and parboiled
salt and freshly ground black pepper
butter

1. Take a 23cm/9 inch frying pan and put into it the onion and 15ml/1 tablespoon oil.

2. Cook slowly over gentle heat until the onion is transparent and soft but not coloured. Remove from the heat.

3. Coarsely grate the potatoes. Season with salt and pepper. Fork in the onion.

4. Heat 15ml/1 tablespoon mixed butter and oil in the frying pan. Add the potato mixture. Pat it lightly into a flat cake with straight sides.

5. Fry gently until the underside is crusty and golden brown (about 15 minutes). Shake the pan every so often to ensure that the cake does not stick.

6. Place a plate larger than the frying pan over the pan and turn both plate and pan over to tip the rösti out on to the plate. Slip it immediately back into the pan to cook the other side for 5 minutes. Place in a warm oven for 15 minutes, if necessary. Serve on a large flat dish, cut into wedges like a cake.

NOTE I: Finely grated raw carrots are sometimes added to the mixture. The potato cake can be baked in the oven at 190°C/375°F/gas mark 5 for about 30 minutes rather than fried.

NOTE II: Very old large floury potatoes need not be parboiled before grating. The boiling is to remove some of the sticky starch present in small young waxy potatoes.

Pommes Anna

SERVES 4

675g/1¹/2lb potatoes, peeled and finely sliced
55g/2oz butter, clarified (see NOTE *below)*
salt and pepper
grated nutmeg

1. Heat the oven to 190°C/375°F/gas mark 5. Brush a heavy ovenproof pan with the butter.

2. Arrange a neat layer of overlapping potato slices on the bottom of the pan. Brush the potatoes with the melted butter and season well with salt, pepper and nutmeg.

3. Continue to layer the potatoes, butter and seasoning until all the potatoes have been used. Finish with butter and seasoning.

4. Hold the pan over direct medium heat for 2 minutes to brown the bottom layer of potatoes.

5. Take off and cover with greased paper and a lid or foil. Bake in the oven for about 45 minutes.

6. When the potatoes are tender, invert a serving plate over the pan and turn the potatoes out so that the neat first layer is now on top.

NOTE: To clarify butter, heat until foaming, then strain through a piece of muslin.

Brussels Sprouts and Chestnuts

SERVES 4

450g/1lb very small Brussels sprouts
225g/8oz fresh chestnuts
45g/1¹/2oz butter
salt, freshly ground black pepper and nutmeg

1. Wash and trim the sprouts, paring the stalks and removing the outside leaves if necessary.

2. Make a slit in the skin of each chestnut and put them into a pan of cold water. Bring to the boil, simmer for 10 minutes and then take off the heat. Remove 1 or 2 nuts at a time and peel. The skins come off easily if the chestnuts are hot but not too cooked.

3. Melt the butter in a frying pan, and slowly fry the chestnuts, which will break up a little, until brown.

4. Bring a large pan of salted water to the boil, and tip in the sprouts. Boil fairly fast until they are cooked, but not soggy: the flavour changes disastrously if boiled too long. Drain them well.

5. Mix the sprouts and chestnuts together gently, adding the butter from the frying pan. Season with salt, pepper and nutmeg.

Provençal Tomatoes

SERVES 4
4 medium tomatoes
55g/2oz butter
1 onion, finely chopped
1/2 garlic clove, crushed
60ml/4 tablespoons stale white breadcrumbs
salt and freshly ground black pepper
pinch of nutmeg
10ml/2 teaspoons chopped fresh parsley
5ml/1 teaspoon chopped tarragon
chopped parsley to garnish

1. Heat the oven to 200°C/400°F/gas mark 6.

2. Cut the tomatoes in half horizontally. Spoon out and strain the tomato pulp.

3. Melt half the butter and gently cook the onion in it until soft. Add the garlic and cook for 1 more minute.

4. Mix the breadcrumbs, seasoning, nutmeg, herbs, and onion mixture together with a fork. Add enough strained tomato to make a wet but not soggy stuffing.

5. Pile the breadcrumb mixture into the tomatoes and place a knob of the remaining butter on each.

6. Put the tomatoes in an ovenproof dish and bake in the oven for about 20 minutes or until the breadcrumbs are golden.

7. Sprinkle with chopped parsley.

Celeriac Purée

SERVES 4
2 medium potatoes
225g/8oz celeriac
290ml/1/2 pint milk
55g/2oz butter
salt and white pepper

1. Wash and peel the potatoes and place them in a pan of cold salted water. Bring to the boil, cover and simmer for about 25 minutes until tender.

2. Meanwhile, wash the celeriac, peel it and cut into chunks. Simmer slowly in the milk for about 20-30 minutes until tender.

3. Mash the celeriac with its milk, which should by now be much reduced.

4. Drain the potatoes and mash or sieve them. Place the potatoes and celeriac together in a pan. Beat over a gentle heat, adding the butter as you mix. Add salt and pepper to taste.

5. Pile into a serving dish and serve at once.

Purée Clamart

SERVES 4
1 medium onion
45g/1¹/₂oz butter
150ml/¹/₄ pint vegetable stock, or water
450g/1lb frozen or podded fresh peas
salt and pepper
225g/8oz mashed potato (see page 62)

1. Chop the onion finely and put it with the butter, stock and peas in a saucepan. Add a little salt and pepper. Cover the saucepan and simmer the ingredients until the peas are tender. If the peas are fresh, or frozen in a solid block, it may be necessary to add a splash more stock during cooking as the cooking time will be longer.

2. Liquidize the peas with any remaining juice, or push through a sieve. Turn into a bowl.

3. Gradually beat the potato into the peas. The purée should be soft but able to hold its shape. Taste for seasoning and turn into a warm dish.

Red Ratatouille

SERVES 4
1 medium aubergine
olive oil
2 red onions, sliced
1 garlic clove, crushed
1 large red pepper, sliced
400g/14oz tin of tomatoes
salt and freshly ground black pepper
crushed coriander
15ml/1 tablespoon chopped purple basil
   (optional)

1. Wipe the aubergine, cut into bite-sized chunks and degorge (sprinkle with salt and leave to drain for about 30 minutes). Rinse away the salt and dry the aubergine well.

2. Heat a little oil in a pan and add the onions and garlic. When soft but not brown, add the aubergine and fry to a pale brown. Add the red pepper and fry for another couple of minutes over a low heat until the pepper softens a little.

3. Add the tinned tomatoes, salt, pepper and a pinch of crushed coriander. Cover with a lid and simmer gently for about 20 minutes until the vegetables have softened but not broken up. (If the ratatouille is too wet, remove the lid and reduce the juices.)

4. Check seasoning and serve sprinkled with chopped purple basil.

Ratatouille

SERVES 2-3 AS A MAIN COURSE
2 small aubergines
2 courgettes
olive oil
1 large onion, sliced
1 garlic clove, crushed
1 medium green pepper, sliced
1 small red pepper, sliced
6 tomatoes, peeled, quartered and deseeded
salt and freshly ground black pepper
pinch of crushed coriander
15ml/1 tablespoon chopped fresh basil
(optional)

1. Wipe the aubergines and courgettes and cut into bite-sized chunks. Degorge (sprinkle with salt and leave to drain for about 30 minutes). Rinse away the salt and dry the vegetables well.

2. Melt a little oil in a pan and add the onions and garlic. When soft but not brown, add the aubergine and fry to a pale brown, adding more oil if necessary. Add the peppers and courgettes, cover and cook gently for 25 minutes.

3. Add the tomatoes, salt if necessary, pepper and coriander. Cook, covered, for about 20 minutes.

4. Dish up and sprinkle with basil. Serve hot or well chilled.

NOTE: If you are making large quantities of ratatouille try this catering trick. Deep-fry the aubergines, peppers and courgettes in oil. Drain them and put into the saucepan with the onions, which you have gently fried in olive oil, and the tomatoes. Cook, covered, for 10 minutes with the flavourings. Deep-frying saves a lot of time, but the oil must be clean.

MEDIUM RED

Vegetable Stew

SERVES 4
110g/4oz haricot beans
55g/2oz butter
3 small whole onions, peeled
2 leeks, washed and cut up
2 courgettes, cut in chunks
2 medium carrots, peeled and cut into chunks
2 sticks celery, cut in chunks
3 small tomatoes, peeled and quartered
290ml/1/2 pint vegetable stock
3 new potatoes, cut into chunks
salt and freshly ground black pepper
1/4 cauliflower, broken into florets
10ml/2 teaspoons flour
10ml/2 teaspoons chopped fresh parsley
10ml/2 teaspoons chopped fresh mint

To serve:
brown rice (see page 60)

1. Soak the haricot beans for 3 hours. Cook them in fresh boiling water until tender, 1-2 hours. Drain well.

2. Melt half the butter, add the onions and cook them slowly for 1 minute, then add the leeks, courgettes, carrots, celery and tomatoes. Pour on the stock and bring to the boil. Add the potatoes, season with salt and pepper and simmer for about 30 minutes. Add the cauliflower and beans and continue to simmer for about 15 minutes until all the vegetables are tender.

3. Mix the remaining butter and the flour to a paste (beurre manié). Slip a little at a time down the side of the pan and into the mixture, stirring gently. When all the beurre manié has been added you should have a smooth, slightly thickened sauce for the vegetables. Simmer the stew for 3 minutes to cook the flour. Add the parsley and mint. Taste and season as required. Serve with brown rice.

MEDIUM RED

Salsify (or Scorzonera) in Mornay Sauce

Salsify and scorzonera are classified as different vegetables but they taste very alike and are treated similarly, the only practical difference being that salsify is peeled before cooking and scorzonera afterwards. In fact both may be peeled before cooking, but the flavour of scorzonera boiled in its skin is said to be superior.

SERVES 2 AS A MAIN COURSE
12 roots salsify or scorzonera
salt
lemon juice (for salsify only)
290ml/ 1/2 pint mornay sauce (see page 140)
grated cheese
dried white breadcrumbs

FOR SALSIFY:

1. Wash, peel and cut each root into 3-4 pieces.

2. Place in a pan with a cupful of salted water with a little lemon juice and simmer, with a tightly closed lid, for 12-20 minutes, or until tender, topping up with water if necessary.

3. Drain well and arrange in a serving dish.

4. Coat with the hot mornay sauce, sprinkle with grated cheese and breadcrumbs and brown under the grill.

FOR SCORZONERA:

1. Wash and cut each root into 3-4 pieces.

2. Place unpeeled into a pan of boiling salted water and simmer until tender, 15-20 minutes.

3. Drain well and peel off the skin.

4. Proceed as for salsify.

MEDIUM RED

Red Cabbage

SERVES 6
1 small red cabbage
1 onion, sliced
30g/1oz butter
1 small cooking apple, peeled and sliced
1 small dessert apple, peeled and sliced
10ml/2 teaspoons brown sugar
10ml/2 teaspoons vinegar
pinch of ground cloves
salt and freshly ground black pepper

1. Shred the cabbage and discard the hard stalks. Rinse well.

2. In a large saucepan, fry the onion in the butter until it begins to soften.

3. Add the drained but still wet cabbage, the apples, sugar, vinegar and cloves, and season with salt and pepper.

4. Cover tightly and cook very slowly, mixing well and stirring every 15 minutes or so. Cook for 2 hours, or until the whole mass is soft and reduced in bulk. (During the cooking it may be necessary to add a little water.)

5. Taste and add more salt, pepper or sugar if necessary.

FULL RED

Lentils with Cloves

SERVES 4
2 large onions, sliced
3 large carrots, sliced
1 garlic clove, crushed
sunflower oil
225g/8oz brown lentils
750ml/1¼ pints vegetable stock (see page 136)
15ml/1 tablespoon tomato purée
15ml/1 tablespoon dried Provençal herbs
6 cloves, tied up in a piece of muslin
black pepper

1. Brown the onions, carrots and garlic in a minimum amount of sunflower oil in a nonstick frying pan.

2. Heat the oven to 170°C/325°F/gas mark 3.

3. Transfer the onion mixture to an ovenproof dish. Add the lentils, stock, tomato purée, herbs and cloves. Bring gradually up to the boil. Stir well and season with pepper.

4. Cook in the preheated oven for 1¼ hours, or until the lentils are just tender and the stock absorbed. Check every so often that all is well – you can never rely completely on a pulse recipe for either cooking times or liquor quantities.

Hot Raw Beetroot

SERVES 4
450g/1lb raw beetroot
55g/2oz butter
salt and coarsely ground black pepper
squeeze of lemon

1. Peel the beetroot and put it through the julienne blade of a processor or grate it on a coarse cheese grater or mandolin.

2. Melt the butter. Toss the beetroot in it for 2 minutes until hot but by no means cooked.

3. Season with salt and pepper and a sprinkle of lemon juice.

NOTE: Raw beetroot in a mustardy vinaigrette is very good too.

Spinach Bhajee

SERVES 2 AS A MAIN COURSE
900g/2lb fresh spinach, cooked and chopped
45ml/3 tablespoons oil
1 medium onion, finely chopped
1 green chilli, deseeded and chopped
1 garlic clove, crushed
2.5cm/1 inch piece root ginger, grated
10ml/2 teaspoons ground coriander
5ml/1 teaspoon ground cumin
6 cardamom pods
1 tomato, deseeded and sliced
salt and freshly ground black pepper

1. Heat the oil and fry the onion until it is golden. Add the chilli, garlic, ginger and spices and cook together for 1 minute.

2. Add the spinach and tomato and stir over a gentle heat for about 6 minutes. Season with salt and pepper. If necessary, boil away any extra liquid.

FULL RED

Cauliflower Fritters

SERVES 2-3 AS A MAIN COURSE
1 large cauliflower
lemon juice
freshly ground black pepper
oil for deep-frying
150ml/¼ pint fritter batter (see page 152)

To serve:
290ml/½ pint tomato sauce (see page 139)

1. Cut the cauliflower into florets. Boil them in salted water for 3 minutes.

2. Drain the florets well. When dry, sprinkle liberally with lemon juice and season with black pepper.

3. Heat the oil until a crumb will sizzle in it.

4. Dip each piece of cauliflower in the seasoned fritter batter and drop carefully into the hot oil.

5. The batter will puff up and the cauliflower is ready when golden brown. Drain well and serve immediately with tomato sauce.

NOTE: This dish is delicious on its own as a lunchtime dish, or as a first course for a more elaborate meal.

DRY WHITE

Zucchini Fritters

SERVES 4
450g/1lb courgettes (zucchini)
flour
salt and freshly ground black pepper
oil for deep-frying
2 egg whites

1. Cut the courgettes into thin chip-like strips. Sprinkle with salt and leave for 30 minutes. Rinse, drain and dry.

2. Season the flour well with salt and pepper.

3. Heat the oil until a crumb will sizzle vigorously in it.

4. Whisk the egg whites until stiff but not dry.

5. Put the courgettes in a sieve. Add the seasoned flour and toss them in it. Then turn them in the egg white.

6. Fry a few at a time until brown. Drain on absorbent paper. Season with salt and pepper. Serve immediately.

ITALIAN DRY WHITE

Vegetable Couscous

Couscous is made from wheat. It is similar to semolina, but coarser. It is available in specialist shops.

SERVES 4
110g/4oz chickpeas
110g/4oz couscous
425ml/³/4 pint vegetable stock (see page 136)
salt and freshly ground black pepper
4 button onions, peeled
2 leeks, coarsely chopped
1 carrot, peeled and coarsely chopped
stick of celery, coarsely chopped
2 courgettes, coarsely chopped
4 tomatoes, peeled and cut into quarters
5ml/1 teaspoon chopped fresh mint
10ml/2 teaspoons chopped fresh parsley
pinch of dried oregano
*pinch of saffron or a few shreds soaked in
    5ml/1 tablespoon water*

For the sauce:
30ml/2 tablespoons hot stock
5ml/1 teaspoon cumin
5ml/1 teaspoon ground coriander
2.5ml/¹/2 teaspoon chilli powder
30ml/2 tablespoons tomato purée

1. Soak the chickpeas for 3 hours. Drain them and simmer for 1-2 hours in fresh salted water until they are tender. Drain well.

2. Cover the couscous with 230ml/8 fl oz cold water and leave to absorb the liquid for 20 minutes.

3. Put the stock, salt, pepper and onions in a large saucepan. Bring slowly to the boil and add the leeks, carrots and celery.

4. Set the couscous to steam in a muslin-lined sieve or couscoussière above the cooking vegetables. Cover the sieve with foil or a cloth to prevent too much steam escaping and simmer for 30 minutes.

5. Add the courgettes to the vegetables. Fork through the couscous to remove any lumps and return the lid. Cook for 2 minutes.

6. Add the tomatoes, mint, parsley and oregano to the vegetable mixture and again cover and cook for 2 minutes. Pour the couscous into a dish and keep warm.

7. Add the chickpeas and saffron, with its water if soaked, to the vegetables, and heat for 2 minutes. Drain off some of the stock.

8. For the sauce, mix the hot stock with the cumin, coriander, chilli powder and tomato purée.

9. Spread the couscous over a flat serving dish and pile the vegetables, with a cupful or so of stock, on the top. Serve the spiced sauce separately.

MEDIUM RED

Mjadara

SERVES 4
225g/8oz brown lentils, soaked for 2 hours
1 litre/2 pints salted water
55g/2oz long-grain rice
30ml/2 tablespoons olive oil or vegetable oil
1 large onion, finely sliced
salt

For the garnish:
raw onion rings, finely sliced
raw tomato, finely sliced

1. Drain the lentils and cook in the salted water for about 1 hour or until just tender but not broken.

2. Add the rice and stir, making sure that there is enough water to cook it. Cook for about 20 minutes until the rice is tender. At the end of the cooking time the water should be absorbed by the rice and lentils. If it is not, boil the mixture rapidly until the liquid is reduced to leave rice and lentils moist but not swimming.

3. While the rice is cooking, heat the oil in a frying pan and cook the onion very slowly until soft and just brown. Pour this into the rice and lentil dish, stir well and season with salt. Transfer to a warmed flat dish. Garnish with the onion and tomato rings.

NOTE: This Middle Eastern peasant dish is good served with a finely sliced cabbage salad dressed with yoghurt, lemon and garlic.

FULL RED

Noodles with Red Peppers

SERVES 4
1 medium red pepper, quartered and deseeded
225g/8oz fettucine noodles
15ml/1 tablespoon olive oil
salt and freshly ground black pepper

1. Grill the pepper until the skin is black and blistered. Cool, remove the skin and slice.

2. Cook the pasta in plenty of rapidly boiling salted water for about 6 minutes, until tender but not too soft. Drain and leave in the colander.

3. Heat the oil, add the peppers and shake over the heat until sizzling. Add the pasta and pile into a warmed serving dish. Season with plenty of pepper.

Carrot and Mint Salad

SERVES 4
8 large carrots
2.5ml/1/2 teaspoon caster sugar
large pinch of cumin powder
French dressing (see page 136)
30ml/2 tablespoons chopped fresh mint

1. Mix the sugar and cumin powder with the dressing.

2. Peel the carrots and grate coarsely into the French dressing.

3. Add the mint and toss the salad well. Taste and season with salt and pepper if necessary.

Fennel and Walnut Salad

SERVES 6
3 small bulbs of fennel
110g/4oz fresh shelled walnuts, coarsely chopped
15ml/1 tablespoon chopped marjoram
French dressing made with hazelnut oil (see page 136)

1. Remove the feathery green tops of the fennel and put aside. Wash, then finely slice the fennel heads, discarding any tough outer leaves or discoloured bits.

2. Blanch the fennel in boiling water for 3-4 minutes to soften slightly. Refresh by running under cold water until cool. Drain well on absorbent paper, or dry in a tea towel.

3. Mix together the fennel, nuts and marjoram and moisten with a little French dressing. Pile into a salad bowl.

4. Chop the green leaves of the fennel and scatter them over the salad.

Fennel, Red Onion and Red Pepper Salad

SERVES 4-6
1 large or 2 small heads fennel
1 red pepper
½ medium-sized red onion, sliced

For the dressing:
15ml/1 tablespoon wine vinegar
45ml/3 tablespoons salad oil
pinch of mustard
salt and freshly ground black pepper

1. Remove the feathery green tops of the fennel and put aside. Finely slice the fennel heads, discarding any tough outer leaves. Blanch in boiling salted water for 1 minute. Refresh under cold running water. Drain well.

2. Remove and discard the seeds and inner pith from the pepper. Cut the flesh into quarters. Place, skin side up, under a very hot grill. Grill until very black. Cool, skin and cut into strips.

3. Mix all the dressing ingredients in a jar, shaking well to form an emulsion.

4. Toss everything in the dressing and tip into a clean salad bowl. Chop the green leaves of the fennel and scatter over the salad.

Japanese-style Cucumber and Carrot Salad

This recipe is by Madhur Jaffrey from *The Taste of Health.*

SERVES 4-6
1 large cucumber
1 small carrot
15ml/1 tablespoon unhulled sesame seeds
30ml/2 tablespoons soy sauce
20ml/2 dessertspoons distilled white vinegar

1. Peel the cucumber and cut it diagonally into wafer-thin, long, oval shapes. Put them in a bowl.

2. Peel the carrot and cut this similarly. Put in the bowl with the cucumber.

3. Put the sesame seeds in a small cast-iron frying pan and place it over a low heat. Cook, shaking the pan, until the sesame seeds begin to brown evenly; it takes just a few minutes. When they start popping, they are ready. You can also spread the sesame seeds out on a tray and roast them under the grill. They should turn just a shade darker.

4. Pour the soy sauce and vinegar over the salad, and mix thoroughly. Sprinkle on the sesame seeds and mix again. Serve immediately

Salad of Roast Tomatoes and Spring Onions

SERVES 4

10 medium-sized ripe plum tomatoes, blanched
    and peeled
olive oil
salt and freshly ground black pepper
sugar to taste
sprig of thyme
30g/1oz butter
1/2 bunch spring onions, trimmed and cleaned,
    cut on the cross

For the dressing:
5ml/1 teaspoon Dijon mustard
10ml/2 teaspoons each of tarragon and white
    wine vinegars
30ml/2 tablespoons olive oil
45ml/3 tablespoons vegetable oil
1/2 bunch flat leaf parsley, chopped, for garnish

1. Preheat the oven to 200°C/400°F/gas mark 6. Cut the tomatoes in half vertically and scoop out the seeds. Drain thoroughly on absorbent paper.

2. Brush a baking sheet with olive oil. Arrange the tomatoes cut side up on the tray. Season with salt and pepper and sugar. Scatter with branches of thyme and drizzle over more olive oil.

3. Roast for 10-15 minutes until the flesh just gives when touched.

4. Arrange 5 tomato halves on each plate, cut side down.

5. Melt the butter in a frying pan and sauté the spring onions for about 2 minutes, scatter around the roasted tomatoes.

6. Whisk the dressing ingredients together, check the seasoning, and drizzle over the tomatoes. Garnish with parsley.

SOAVE

Watercress Salad with Croûtons

SERVES 4-5
oil for deep-frying
4 slices white bread, crusts removed, cubed
2 bunches watercress, trimmed

For the dressing:
45ml/3 tablespoons oil
15ml/1 tablespoon vinegar
salt and pepper
1/2 garlic clove, crushed
5ml/1 teaspoon chopped fresh parsley
pinch of sugar (optional)

1. Combine all the dressing ingredients in a screw-top jar and shake well.

2. Make the croûtons: heat the oil until a crumb will sizzle vigorously in it. Fry the bread until golden brown and crisp. Drain well on absorbent paper. Sprinkle lightly with salt.

3. Just before serving toss the watercress in the French dressing, tip into a clean salad bowl and sprinkle the warm croûtons on top.

Red Pepper Salad

SERVES 4
4 red peppers
1 clove garlic
2.5ml/1/2 teaspoon salt
45ml/3 tablespoons extra virgin olive oil
5ml/1 teaspoon chopped fresh oregano
45ml/3 tablespoons stoned black olives

1. Preheat the grill to its highest setting. Cut the peppers into quarters and remove the seeds and any pith. Grill the skin side of the peppers until they are blistered and blackened all over. Place under running cold water and remove the skins. Cut the peppers into strips.

2. Crush the clove of garlic with the salt, add the olive oil and mash well together. Add the oregano and toss in the red pepper strips. Mix with the black olives.

Pasta and Red Pepper Salad

SERVES 3 AS A MAIN COURSE
225g/8oz pasta, preferably spirals
2 red peppers
110g/4oz broccoli
French dressing (see page 136)
chopped sage

1. Cook the pasta in plenty of boiling salted water with 15ml/1 tablespoon oil. When tender drain well and leave to cool.

2. Cut the peppers into quarters and remove the stalk, inner membrane and seeds. Heat the grill to its highest temperature.

3. Grill the peppers, skin side uppermost, until the skin is black and blistered. With a small knife, remove all the skin. Cut into strips.

4. Cook the broccoli in boiling salted water. Refresh under cold running water. Drain well and leave to cool.

5. Toss the pasta, pepper, broccoli, French dressing and sage together.

DRY WHITE WINE

Grilled Radicchio Salad

SERVES 4
2 large radicchio, cut into 8 wedges each

For the dressing:
45ml/3 tablespoons hazelnut or walnut oil
15ml/1 tablespoon balsamic, sherry or
    raspberry vinegar
chopped chives

1. Preheat the grill.

2. Toss the radicchio in the dressing.

3. Grill half of the wedges until brown around the edges but pink in the middle.

4. Toss the grilled radicchio with the ungrilled radicchio and add the chives. Serve immediately.

Quinoa and Lime Salad

SERVES 4-6 AS A MAIN COURSE
255g/9oz quinoa
720ml/1¼ pints water
salt

For the dressing:
juice of 6 limes
125ml/4 fl oz groundnut oil
Salt and freshly ground black pepper
15ml/1 tablespoon sugar
15ml/1 tablespoon dry-roasted Szechuan
*   peppercorns, ground*
4 small garlic cloves, crushed
15ml/1 tablespoon each flat parsley, basil and
coriander

To serve:
10 Kalamata olives, stoned and slivered
140g/5oz cooked kidney beans
1 radicchio
small bunch basil or coriander

1. Rinse and drain the quinoa well before use to remove bitterness. It can then be lightly toasted in oil to enhance the flavour, if you wish.

2. Put the quinoa in a pan with the water and salt, bring to the boil then reduce the heat, cover and cook for 15-20 minutes or until the liquid has been absorbed and the quinoa looks transparent. If all the liquid has not been absorbed, drain well.

3. Remove from the heat and fluff up with a fork. Allow to cool.

4. Make the dressing: put the ingredients into a liquidizer and blend until smooth, then season well to make a strong dressing.

5. Mix the dressing with the quinoa and mix in most of the olives and the kidney beans, reserving a few for garnish.

6. Line a serving bowl with the radicchio leaves, spoon in the quinoa, scatter over the reserved olives and kidney beans and garnish with either fresh basil or coriander.

NOTE I: Quinoa is a grain similar to tapioca. It is available in large supermarkets and health food shops.

NOTE II: This dressing is also very good served with hot or cold pasta. It should not be made the day before it is served as it looses some of its brilliant green colour.

Barley and Beetroot Salad

SERVES 2 AS A MAIN COURSE
30g/1oz barley
1 large beetroot, cooked and chopped
1/2 small onion, very finely chopped
1/2 green apple, chopped
French dressing (see page 136)
110g/4oz lettuce or white cabbage, shredded

1. Boil the barley in plenty of salted water for about 1 hour, until tender. Drain well.

2. Toss the barley with the beetroot, onion and apple in the French dressing. Serve on a bed of shredded lettuce.

Seaweed

This recipe has been adapted from Yan Kit So's excellent *Classic Chinese* cookbook. She says: 'This Northern dish uses a special kind of seaweed which is not available elsewhere. However, the adapted ingredients used below do produce the desired delicious result.'

SERVES 4
450g/1lb spring greens
oil for deep-frying
2.5ml/1/4 teaspoon salt
10ml/2 teaspoons sugar

1. Remove and discard the tough stalks from the spring greens. Wash, then lay them out on a large tray to dry thoroughly.

2. Fold 6-7 leaves, or however many you can handle at a time, into a neat roll and, using a sharp knife, slice very finely into shreds. Lay out on the tray again to dry. The drier the better.

3. Heat a deep-fat fryer until a cube of stale bread will brown in 40 seconds. Add half the spring greens and fry for 30 seconds or until bright green and crisp. Remove with a large strainer and deep-fry the remaining spring greens.

4. Sprinkle with salt and sugar and mix thoroughly.

Main Courses

Wild Mushrooms in a Cage

This recipe has been adapted from one of Paul Gayler's recipes in *Take Six Cooks*.

SERVES 4

For the vegetable stock:
100g/3¹/₂oz unsalted butter
¹/₄ onion, peeled and diced
¹/₂ leek, cleaned and diced
¹/₂ celery stick, diced
30g/1oz carrots, peeled and diced
30g/1oz cabbage, shredded
1.25ml/¹/₄ teaspoon crushed garlic
1.25ml/¹/₄ teaspoon crushed black peppercorns
5ml/1 teaspoon sea salt
150ml/¹/₄ pint white wine
290ml/¹/₂ pint water
30ml/2 tablespoons double cream

4 slices wholemeal bread
45g/1¹/₂oz unsalted butter
2 shallots, finely chopped
100g/3¹/₂oz selection of wild mushrooms,
*   e. g. morels, trompettes, oyster, chanterelles,*
*   etc., washed and roughly chopped if large*
70ml/2¹/₂ fl oz Madeira
70ml/2¹/₂ fl oz white wine
150ml/¹/₄ pint double cream
salt and freshly ground black pepper
100g/3¹/₂oz puff pastry
beaten egg for egg wash

To garnish:
chervil leaves

1. Set the oven to 200°C/400°F/gas mark 6.

2. First prepare the vegetable stock: melt 30g/1oz of the butter in a medium-sized saucepan and add the diced vegetables and garlic. Sweat gently, covered with a lid, for about 5 minutes or until soft. Add the peppercorns, salt and wine. Bring to the boil and simmer, without a lid, until reduced by half.

3. Add the water and bring to the boil, skimming frequently. Simmer gently for 20-25 minutes. Pass through a fine sieve. Skim off any fat that rises to the top and keep until required.

4. Cut out 4 x 9cm/3¹/₂ inch diameter circles of wholemeal bread. Brush with 30g/1oz melted butter and place in a patty tin. Press another patty tin, of the same size, on top and place in the oven for 10 minutes. Remove the top tin and continue to dry out the croustades in the oven.

5. Melt 15g/¹/₂oz of the butter in a sauté pan, add the shallots and cook gently for 2 minutes. Then add the wild mushrooms and continue cooking for 1 minute. Add the Madeira and white wine and cook until reduced by half, then add the cream and continue reducing until the mushrooms are coated with the cream. Then adjust the seasoning and allow to cool.

6. Fill the croustades with the mushroom mixture.

7. Roll out the pastry very thinly and cut out 4 circles 6.5cm/2^1/$_2$ inches in diameter. Make 1cm/^{1}/$_2$ inch parallel gashes into the pastry at regular intervals across the diameter.

8. Brush the pastry with egg wash and put on top of the mushrooms, pulling downwards to stick on the croustade. Rest the pastry in the refrigerator for 30 minutes.

9. Brush the 'cages' with egg wash and place in the preheated oven for 5-8 minutes.

10. Make a sauce from the vegetable stock: cook the stock until reduced by half, add the double cream and reduce again until thickened. Whisk in the remaining butter, adding a little at a time to form an emulsion. Adjust the seasoning.

11. To serve: pour a little sauce on to a serving plate, remove the 'cages' from the oven and place on the centre of the plate. Garnish with the chervil. Serve immediately.

CRISP DRY WHITE

Walnut and Buckwheat Croquettes

SERVES 4
225g/8oz cooked buckwheat
110g/4oz walnuts, broken
4 garlic cloves, crushed
10ml/2 teaspoons oregano
1 egg, beaten
salt and freshly ground black pepper
wholewheat breadcrumbs, toasted
oil for frying

1. Mix all the ingredients, except the breadcrumbs and oil, together, and mould into croquette shapes. Roll in breadcrumbs and refrigerate for 30 minutes. Fry gently in oil over a medium heat.

CRISP DRY WHITE

Exotic Vegetable Couscous

225g/8oz couscous
425ml/³/4 pint tomato juice
425ml/³/4 pint water
1 garlic clove, crushed
5ml/1 teaspoon ground cumin
few sprigs of coriander
salt and freshly ground black pepper

For the vegetables:
10 baby carrots, scraped, with a little green
*   left on*
10 baby turnips, scraped, with a little green
*   left on*
10 fresh okra pods, trimmed
10 ears fresh baby corn
6 tiny purple finger aubergines (if available)
10 pearl onions, skinned
225g/8oz thin asparagus, trimmed

For the sauce:
5ml/1 teaspoon ground cumin
5ml/1 teaspoon ground coriander
2.5ml/¹/2 teaspoon chilli powder
30ml/2 tablespoons tomato purée

1. Cover the couscous with cold water and leave to absorb the liquid for 20 minutes.

2. Put the tomato juice, water, garlic, cumin, coriander, salt and pepper into a large saucepan. Bring up to the boil and simmer for 15 minutes. Strain and return to the saucepan.

3. Set the couscous to steam above the tomato sauce. Ideally it should be put into a muslin-lined steamer or special couscoussière, but a wire sieve lined with a 'J' cloth will do. Put the sieve in place and cover with a pan lid or cloth to prevent the steam escaping too much. Simmer for 20 minutes.

4. Fork the couscous to remove any lumps. Add all the vegetables, except the asparagus, to the tomato sauce and simmer for 5 minutes. Add the asparagus and simmer for a further 5 minutes.

5. Pile the couscous on to a dish and keep warm. Do not worry if it feels a little tacky; it always does.

6. Drain the vegetables, reserving the liquor, and arrange them on top of the couscous. Drizzle over 30ml/2 tablespoons of the tomato sauce. Garnish with the fresh coriander leaves.

7. Mix the remaining tomato sauce with the sauce ingredients and serve it separately. It is very hot.

DRY WHITE

Pizza

This recipe has been taken from *A Taste of Venice* by Jeanette Nance Nordio.

MAKES TWO 25CM/10 INCH PIZZAS
10g/¹/₃ oz fresh yeast
pinch of sugar
150ml/¹/₄ pint lukewarm water
200g/7oz plain flour
2.5ml/¹/₂ teaspoon salt
60-75ml/4-5 tablespoons olive oil
190ml/¹/₃ pint pizzaiola sauce (see
*   page 138)*
225g/8oz mozzarella, diced or grated
45ml/3 tablespoons grated Parmesan cheese

1. Cream the fresh yeast with a pinch of sugar and 30ml/2 tablespoons of the lukewarm water.

2. Sift the flour with the salt and make a well in the centre. Pour in the yeast mixture, the remaining water and the oil. Mix together until it turns into a soft but not wet dough. Add more water or flour if necessary.

3. Turn out on to a floured surface and knead well for about 5 minutes until the dough is smooth. Place in a clean bowl and cover with greased polythene. Leave in a warm place until the dough has doubled in bulk.

4. Preheat the oven to 230°C/450°F/gas mark 8. Divide the dough in 2. Roll each piece into a circle about 25cm/10 inches across. Place on greased and floured baking trays.

5. Crimp or flute the edges slightly to help keep in the filling. Spread with the tomato sauce. Sprinkle with the cheese and pour over a little oil. The pizzas can 'sit' for up to an hour before they are baked.

6. Bake near the bottom of the oven for 5 minutes and then reduce the temperature to 200°C/400°F/gas mark 6 for a further 15 minutes.

LIGHT/MEDIUM RED

Chicago Pizza Pie

It is essential that the tinned tomatoes are very well drained.

MAKES TWO 20CM/8 INCH PIZZAS
5ml/1 teaspoon fresh yeast
290ml/¹/₂ pint lukewarm water
450g/1lb plain flour
2.5ml/¹/₂ teaspoon salt
30ml/2 tablespoons olive oil
225g/8oz mozzarella cheese, thinly sliced
60ml/4 tablespoons tomato purée
good pinch of oregano or marjoram
15ml/1 tablespoon chopped basil
900g/2lb tin Italian tomatoes, very well drained
110g/4oz Italian sausage or salami, chopped
salt and freshly ground black pepper

1. Dissolve the yeast in the lukewarm water. Sift the flour and the salt together and mix to a soft dough with the yeasty water. Mix in the olive oil with a knife and then knead for 10 minutes until elastic and smooth.

2. Grease 2 deep sandwich tins or flan tins with a little more olive oil and divide the dough between the tins. Put in a warm place, such as the airing cupboard, for about 1 hour to rise, then push the dough flat on the bottom of the tins and press to come up the sides. Heat the oven to 250°C/500°F/gas mark 9.

3. Cover the dough with half the mozzarella cheese and put the tins back in the warm place to rise again. When puffy, after about half an hour, push the dough again with the back of a large spoon and once again press the edges up the sides of the tins.

4. Mix the tomato purée, marjoram and basil together and spread this all over the dough. Cut each tinned tomato in half and discard the juice. Put them into the pizzas. Add the rest of the mozzarella cheese and the salami. Sprinkle with a little more marjoram, season well and bake for 20 minutes.

MEDIUM RED

Roman-style Grilled Mozzarella Cheese

2 thin sticks of Italian bread
4 x 110g/4oz packets mozzarella cheese
45ml/3 tablespoons olive oil
salt and freshly ground black pepper
55g/2oz unsalted butter

1. Cut the bread and the mozzarella cheese into 2cm/³/₄ inch thick slices.

2. Preheat the grill to its highest temperature.

3. Skewer the bread alternately with the cheese on 4 short skewers.

4. Pack the bread and cheese really closely together.

5. Place the skewers on an oiled baking sheet.

6. Brush the slices of bread liberally with the olive oil and season with salt and pepper.

7. Lower the grill temperature slightly and grill for 6-8 minutes, turning occasionally, making sure that the bread doesn't burn.

8. Meanwhile, melt the butter in a small saucepan.

9. Remove the skewers from the grill, place on a large flat serving dish, and pour some butter over each skewer.

DRY WHITE

Bocconcini di Parma

SERVES 4-6
16 pancakes (see page 152), made with a pinch
  of nutmeg added to the batter
900g/2lb ricotta cheese
4 egg yolks
1 whole egg
170g/6oz freshly grated Parmesan cheese
55g/2oz butter, softened
freshly grated nutmeg
salt and freshly ground black pepper

1. Drain the ricotta and put it in a bowl. Using a wooden spoon, start to break it up, adding the egg yolks, egg, Parmesan cheese and butter. Mix well and season to taste with nutmeg, salt and pepper. Refrigerate for half an hour.

2. Place a pancake on a board and spread 3 heaped tablespoons of the stuffing along one side. Roll it up. Place the rolled pancake, seam side down, on a baking sheet. Repeat until all the pancakes are stuffed. Refrigerate for half an hour.

3. Preheat the oven to 190°C/375°F/gas mark 5.

4. Grease a 33 x 22cm/13¹/₂ x 8 inch baking dish with butter. Using a very sharp knife cut each pancake into thirds. Arrange them standing up in the baking dish, side by side. Bake for 20 minutes and serve hot.

DRY WHITE

Stuffed Peppers

SERVES 4
4 green or red peppers
30g/1oz butter
1 medium onion, finely diced
1 garlic clove, crushed
110g/4oz mushrooms, finely sliced
30g/1oz split blanched almonds
140g/5oz long-grain rice
290ml/½ pint vegetable stock (see page 136)
5ml/1 teaspoon chopped rosemary
30g/1oz raisins
15ml/1 tablespoon chopped parsley
salt and pepper
290ml/½ pint tomato sauce (see page 139)

1. Cut off the tops of the peppers and remove the core and seeds. Then drop into boiling water for 5 minutes. Plunge immediately into cold water to cool.

2. Set the oven to 190°C/375°F/gas mark 5. Melt the butter in an ovenproof casserole and cook the onion until transparent. Add the garlic, mushrooms and almonds. Sauté (fry briskly, while tossing the contents of the pan in the butter) for a further 2 minutes. Stir in the rice and fry for a further minute.

3. Pour on the stock and bring to the boil. Add the rosemary, raisins, parsley and seasoning. Cover and bake in the oven for 20 minutes. When the rice is cooked, fill the peppers with it and place in a deep ovenproof dish. Pour on the tomato sauce. Cover with wet greaseproof paper and a lid and put back into the oven for 30 minutes.

LIGHT RED

Vegetable Mornay

SERVES 6
1 small cauliflower
salt
225g/8oz shelled peas, or 1 small packet frozen peas
450g/1lb carrots, peeled and cut into batons
3 tomatoes, skinned and halved
570ml/1 pint mornay sauce (see page 139)

To finish:
dry white breadcrumbs
grated cheese

1. Break the cauliflower into sprigs and cook them in boiling salted water until just tender, but not soft.

2. Boil the peas. Boil the carrots in salted water until just tender. Heat the oven to 230°C/450°F/gas mark 8.

3. Put all of the vegetables into an ovenproof dish.

4. Heat the mornay sauce and pour it over the vegetables. Sprinkle with the breadcrumbs and cheese.

5. Bake the vegetables until bubbling and brown on top. If necessary, the finished dish can be briefly grilled.

Hot Sweet Potato Stew

SERVES 4
120ml/4 fl oz oil
15ml/1 tablespoon yellow mustard seeds
5ml/1 teaspoon ground mace
2 green chillies, chopped
5 garlic cloves, crushed
30g/1oz root ginger, peeled and sliced
2 onions, peeled and sliced
225g/8oz sweet potatoes, sliced
225g/8oz parsnip, sliced
450g/1lb chopped tomatoes, or 400g/14oz
    tinned, chopped
15ml/1 tablespoon garam masala
lemon juice to taste
salt and freshly ground black pepper

1. Heat the oil in a large pan, add the mustard seeds and mace and cook until the seeds pop.

2. Reduce the heat, add the chilli, garlic, ginger and onion, and fry gently.

3. Add the sweet potato, parsnip and tomatoes. Cover and simmer very gently until the vegetables soften. Add the garam masala. Season to taste with lemon juice, salt and pepper.

MEDIUM DRY WHITE

Risotto alla Milanese

SERVES 4
85g/3oz unsalted butter
1 large onion, finely chopped
400g/14oz risotto rice (arborio)
150ml/1/4 pint white wine
1.75 litres/3 pints vegetable stock (see page 136)
about 15 saffron filaments
salt and freshly ground pepper
30g/1oz unsalted butter
55g/2oz freshly grated Parmesan cheese

1. Melt the butter in a large saucepan and gently cook the onion until soft and lightly coloured. Add the rice and the wine, bring to the boil and cook until the wine is absorbed, about 3 minutes. Stir gently all the time.

2. Meanwhile, in a second pan reheat the stock and add the saffron filaments to it. Let the stock simmer gently.

3. Start adding the hot stock to the rice a little at a time, stirring gently. Allow the stock to become absorbed between each addition. Keep stirring constantly. Season with salt and pepper, and keep adding the stock until the rice is cooked but still al dente, about 20 minutes. Then remove the pan from the heat, add the butter and the Parmesan cheese and mix well with a wooden spoon until the butter is melted and the cheese absorbed. Serve straight away, with additional Parmesan if desired.

LIGHT RED

Risotto with Three Cheeses

SERVES 4-6
110g/4oz Gorgonzola, crust removed
110g/4oz mozzarella cheese
150ml/¼ pint lukewarm milk
85g/3oz butter
15ml/1 tablespoon olive oil
450g/1lb arborio rice
860ml/1½ pints vegetable stock (see page 136)
salt and freshly ground black pepper
30 shelled pistachio nuts, blanched and skinned
   (or use toasted pinenuts)
110g/4oz freshly grated Parmesan cheese

1. Cut the Gorgonzola and mozzarella into small cubes. Place in a bowl, pour over the milk and leave to stand for 20 minutes.

2. Heat the butter and oil in a flameproof casserole over a medium heat. When the butter is melted, add the rice and cook very slowly for 4 minutes.

3. Meanwhile, heat the stock and gradually add it to the rice, stirring continuously and gently until all the stock has been absorbed, taking about 15 minutes.

4. Add the milk with the cheeses to the pan and stir continuously until amalgamated. This will take about 5 minutes. Then taste for seasoning and add the pistachio nuts and Parmesan cheese. Serve.

NOTE: This risotto has to be made at the last minute as it does not keep warm well.

LIGHT RED

Pasta with Tomato and Egg Sauce

SERVES 4
2 large Spanish onions, sliced
15ml/1 tablespoon olive oil
2 x 400g/14oz tins of tomatoes, chopped
salt and pepper
285g/10oz pasta butterflies or spirals
15ml/1 tablespoon chopped fresh basil
3 eggs, beaten lightly
freshly grated Parmesan cheese

1. Cook the onions very slowly in the olive oil until soft but not coloured – this should take 15-20 minutes.

2. Add the tomatoes, salt and pepper, stir well and bring the mixture up to the boil. Let it simmer for 10 minutes.

3. Meanwhile, cook the pasta in rapidly boiling water to which 5ml/1 teaspoon of oil and a little salt has been added. When the pasta is cooked, drain it well and refresh with hot water.

4. Take the tomato sauce off the heat, season it, add the basil and then gradually pour in the lightly beaten eggs. The sauce should become rich and creamy.

5. Mix a little of the sauce with the pasta, pile it into a serving dish and pour the remaining sauce over it.

6. Serve sprinkled with a little freshly grated Parmesan cheese.

MEDIUM RED

Spaghetti en Papillote

This is an unusual way to serve spaghetti but it keeps it moist and succulent.

SERVES 4
150ml/¼ pint good-quality olive oil
1 large garlic clove, peeled
400g/14oz tin Italian tomatoes, drained
salt and freshly ground black pepper
1.25ml/¼ teaspoon chilli powder
225g/8oz spaghetti
*450g/1lb fresh tomatoes, skinned, deseeded
    and slivered*
30ml/2 tablespoons finely chopped parsley
28 large black Greek olives, pitted

1. Heat all but 30ml/2 tablespoons of the oil in a heavy saucepan. When warm, add the garlic and leave to infuse over a gentle heat for 2 minutes. Remove and add the drained tomatoes, taking care as the oil will spit. Simmer for 20 minutes, stirring occasionally. Season with salt, pepper and the chilli powder.

2. Process or liquidize until smooth and return to the rinsed-out saucepan. Simmer for a further 10 minutes until it reduces to a thick shiny sauce.

3. Set the oven to 190°C/375°F/gas mark 5.

4. Cook the spaghetti in plenty of fast-boiling salted water with 15ml/1 tablespoon oil until just tender.

5. While the spaghetti is cooking, arrange 4 x 30cm/12 inch circles of double greaseproof paper on a board.

6. Drain the spaghetti, mix it with the fresh tomatoes, the remaining oil, half the parsley, the olives and the tomato sauce. Mix well and season to taste if necessary.

7. Divide the spaghetti mixture between the 4 circles of greaseproof paper. Close each parcel up, trap a little air in the parcel and secure the edges firmly by twisting and turning them together.

8. Place in a shallow, wet roasting pan and bake for 15 minutes.

9. Remove from the oven and place on warm individual plates. Open the parcels with scissors and sprinkle the remaining parsley over each serving.

MEDIUM RED

Greek Parsley Pasta

SERVES 4
1 batch 3-egg pasta (see page 152)
1 bunch Greek parsley
pesto sauce (see page 145)

1. Roll the pasta out, very thinly, on a lightly floured board. Roll to a rectangle. Cut in half. Keep well covered to prevent it drying out.

2. Take one sheet of pasta and arrange individual parsley leaves at 3cm/1¹/2 inch intervals, in even rows, all over it. Cover loosely with the other sheet of pasta and press down firmly. Roll again until the Greek parsley can be seen between the layers of pasta.

3. Using a pastry cutter, cut between the rows, making sure that all the edges are sealed.

4. Simmer in boiling salted water for 2-3 minutes or until just tender. Drain well and toss in warm pesto sauce.

MEDIUM RED

Pasta Roulade with Tomato Sauce

SERVES 4
1kg/2lb spinach, cooked and chopped
30g/1oz butter
225g/8oz ricotta cheese
85g/3oz toasted pinenuts
nutmeg
salt and freshly ground black pepper
15ml/1 tablespoon roughly chopped fresh basil
1 batch 3-egg pasta (see page 152)

To serve:
fresh tomato sauce (see page 139)
freshly grated Parmesan cheese

1. Melt the butter in a saucepan, add the spinach and cook for 1 minute, stirring continuously to prevent sticking. Add the ricotta, pinenuts, seasonings and basil. Leave to cool.

2. Roll out the pasta into a large thin circle. Spread the spinach filling evenly over the surface, then roll up like a Swiss roll. Wrap the roll in a clean 'J' cloth or muslin and tie the ends with string, like a cracker.

3. Cook in a large saucepan or fish kettle of salted simmering water for approximately 20 minutes.

4. Set the oven to 200°C/400°F/gas mark 6. Slice thickly and arrange in an ovenproof dish. Pour over the tomato sauce, scatter over the Parmesan cheese and reheat in the oven for 20 minutes.

MEDIUM RED

Ravioli with Spinach and Ricotta Filling

SERVES 4

egg pasta made with 340g/12oz flour (see
  page 152)

For the filling:
450g/1lb spinach, cooked and choppped
110g/4oz ricotta cheese
1 egg
salt and freshly ground black pepper
grated nutmeg
freshly grated Parmesan cheese

To serve:
pesto sauce (see page 145)

1. Mix the spinach with the ricotta cheese and beat well with the egg. Season to taste with salt, pepper, nutmeg and Parmesan cheese.

2. Roll the pasta into a very thin rectangle. Cut accurately in half. Keep well covered to prevent drying out.

3. Take one sheet of pasta and place half-teaspoons of filling, in even rows, all over it. Brush round the piles of filling with a little water. Cover loosely with the other sheet of pasta and press firmly round each mound of filling. Check carefully that you have no bubbles of air.

4. Cut between the rows, making sure that all the edges are sealed. Allow to dry on a wire rack for 30 minutes.

5. Simmer for 6-10 minutes until tender. Drain well and serve with the pesto sauce.

BARDOLINO OR VALPOLICELLA

Lemon and Garlic Gnocchi with Warm Borlotti Beans

SERVES 4

1 batch well-seasoned gnocchi (see page 55)
3 cloves garlic, unpeeled
oil
110g/4oz fine white breadcrumbs
1 lemon, finely grated
45ml/3 tablespoons chopped parsley
freshly ground black pepper
1 beaten egg

To serve:
oil for frying
2 x 400g/14oz tins borlotti beans, drained
150ml/¼ pint extra virgin olive oil
2 garlic cloves, peeled
1 small red chilli, deseeded
30ml/2 tablespoons chopped basil
juice of 1 lemon
salt and freshly ground black pepper

1. Preheat oven to 400°F/200°C/gas mark 6.

2. Make the gnocchi and leave to chill in a shallow square tin which has been rinsed with water.

3. Paint the 3 cloves of garlic with a little oil and cook, about 10 minutes, peel and crush.

4. Mix together the garlic, breadcrumbs, lemon rind and parsley, season with black pepper.

5. Divide the chilled gnocchi into 8 even pieces. Dip into beaten egg and then coat evenly in the breadcrumbs.

6. Heat enough oil in a frying pan to come half-way up the gnocchi, fry until golden brown on both sides. Drain well and keep warm in the oven.

7. Meanwhile heat the virgin olive oil, remove from the heat, add the garlic and chilli and leave to infuse for a ½ hour. Strain.

8. Heat the infused oil and when hot, quickly fry the basil. When it turns bright green reduce the heat, add the borlotti beans and heat through, add the lemon juice, salt and pepper to taste.

9. Divide the warmed beans between four warm plates, and put 2 gnocchi on each plate.

SPICY DRY WHITE

Above: Herb Omelette Salad.

Left: Aubergine Loaf. Above: Marinated Italian Aubergines and Courgettes.
Overleaf: Red Pepper Bavarois with Red Pepper Salad.

Above: Salad of Roast Tomatoes and Spring Onions.
Previous Page: Terrine de Ratatouille Niçoise.

Above: Pizza.

Above: Greek Parsley Pasta.
Right: Caroline's Ricotta Pie.

Above: Aubergine Charlotte.

Above: Wild Mushrooms. 1. St George. 2. Velvet shank. 3. Blackening Russula. 4. Cep. 5. Wood blewit. 6. Shiitake. 7. Oyster (pink). 8. Oyster (yellow). 9. Chanterelle. 10 Oyster (wild). 11 Morel. 12. Fairy Ring Champignon.

Above: Black Coffee Jelly with Greek Yoghurt.

Above: Arranged Fruit Salad.

Left: Summer Pudding. Above: Raspberries and Fromage Blanc with Fresh Figs.
Overleaf: Brandy Snap Tortes.

Tagliatelle with Oyster Mushrooms and Sage

SERVES 3
225g/8oz tagliatelle
oil
salt and freshly ground pepper
55g/2oz butter
450g/1lb oyster mushrooms, sliced
15ml/1 tablespoon chopped sage

1. Cook the tagliatelle in plenty of boiling salted water, to which 15ml/1 tablespoon of oil has been added, until tender. Drain well and keep warm.

2. Melt the butter in a large saucepan and cook the oyster mushrooms for 1-2 minutes until soft. Add the tagliatelle and sage, season to taste with salt and pepper and serve immediately.

DRY WHITE

Tricolour Pasta Salad

SERVES 4
225g/8oz pasta twists
1 red pepper, deseeded and quartered
450g/1lb broccoli
90ml/6 tablespoons French dressing (see page 136)
30ml/2 tablespoons chopped parsley

1. Cook the pasta in plenty of boiling salted water until just tender. Rinse under running water until completely cold and drain well.

2. Grill the pepper until the skin is well charred, scrape off the skin and cut the flesh into 5mm/1/4 inch wide strips.

3. Cut the broccoli into small florets and cook in boiling water for 1 minute. Rinse under cold water and drain well.

4. Toss the pasta, peppers and broccoli in the French dressing and parsley. Serve chilled.

LIGHT DRY WHITE

Potato Tart

This doesn't sound very exciting but is in fact a truly delicious tart.

SERVES 6-8
225g/8oz plain flour
pinch of salt
110g/4oz butter
1 egg yolk
very cold water

For the tomato filling:
45ml/3 tablespoons olive oil
1 onion, finely chopped
8 medium tomatoes, peeled, deseeded and
  chopped
15ml/1 tablespoon tomato purée
1 sprig thyme
pinch of sugar
salt and freshly ground black pepper

For the potato filling:
6 waxy potatoes, peeled and cut into even
  chunks
30ml/2 tablespoons olive oil

For the onion filling:
85g/3oz unsalted butter
5 medium onions, thinly sliced

To serve:
150ml/¼ pint crème fraîche
freshly grated nutmeg

1. Set the oven to 200°C/400°F/gas mark 6.

2. Sift the flour with the salt. Then rub in the fats until the mixture looks like breadcrumbs.

3. Mix the yolk with 45ml/3 tablespoons water and add to the mixture. Mix to a firm dough, first with a knife and then with one hand, adding more water if necessary.

4. Roll the pastry out and line a 23cm/9 inch flan ring. Chill in the refrigerator for 20 minutes and then bake blind (see page 152) for 15 minutes in the preheated oven.

5. To make the tomato filling, heat the oil over a low heat and cook the onion gently for about 10 minutes. Add the tomatoes, tomato purée, thyme, sugar, salt and pepper. Increase the heat and cook until all the liquid evaporates. This will take about 35 minutes.

6. Brush the potatoes with oil and sprinkle with salt. Roast in the preheated oven until tender, about 1 hour. Cut into 5mm/¼ inch slices. Turn the oven up to 230°C/450°F/gas mark 6.

7. To make the onion filling: melt the butter, add the onions and cook slowly until soft and creamy – about 30 minutes.

8. Spread the onions on the pastry base and cover with the tomato filling, then arrange the sliced potatoes around the top. Cover with crème fraîche and sprinkle with nutmeg. Bake in the preheated oven for 6-7 minutes or until brown. Serve at room temperature.

LIGHT RED

Cheese and Nut Balls

SERVES 6
110g/4oz fresh brown breadcrumbs
85g/3oz chopped mixed nuts, e.g. hazelnuts,
almonds, walnuts, toasted
15ml/1 tablespoon chopped mixed herbs, e.g.
parsley, mint, thyme
1 large onion, finely chopped
5ml/1 teaspoon tomato purée
110g/4oz Cheddar cheese, grated
1 egg lightly beaten
salt and freshly ground pepper
seasoned flour
oil for frying

1. Mix together all the ingredients except the flour. Season well with salt and plenty of freshly ground black pepper.

2. Using wet hands shape the mixture into balls the size of a ping pong ball, roll in seasoned flour and deep-fry in oil until brown.

LIGHT RED

Caroline's Ricotta Pie

Caroline Yates is on the staff at Leith's and sometimes cooks us the most perfect vegetarian lunches. This is one of her most popular recipes.

For the 'pie':
840g/1¾lb ricotta cheese
4 egg yolks
1 egg
170g/6oz fresh Parmesan cheese, grated
55g/2oz unsalted butter, softened
salt and freshly ground black pepper
grated nutmeg

To serve:
pesto sauce (see page 145)

1. Set the oven to 190°C/375°F/gas mark 5.

2. Mix together the ricotta, egg yolks, egg, Parmesan cheese and butter. Beat well and season to taste with salt, pepper and nutmeg.

3. Turn into a buttered 1 litre/2 pint ovenproof dish.

4. Bake for 30 minutes. Cool slightly. Turn out on to a plate. Drizzle with the pesto sauce and serve while still warm.

MEDIUM RED

Aubergine Charlotte

This is a useful supper dish – a layered up aubergine and tomato 'pie' which is good served with a crisp green salad and Basmati rice.

SERVES 4
4 large aubergines
salt and freshly ground black pepper
1 onion, finely chopped
olive oil
1 garlic clove, crushed
15 tomatoes, peeled, deseeded and chopped
290ml/¹/₂ pint yoghurt
vegetable stock (see page 136)

1. Slice and salt the aubergines and leave to 'degorge' in a colander for 30 minutes. Meanwhile, cook the onion in a little oil for 3 minutes. Add the garlic, tomatoes, salt and pepper and cook for a further 25 minutes.

2. Rinse and dry the aubergines. Steam for 20 minutes.

3. Set the oven to 180°C/350°F/gas mark 4.

4. Arrange a layer of aubergine slices along the bottom and up the sides of a loaf or Charlotte tin.

5. Layer up two-thirds of the tomatoes, the yoghurt and remaining aubergines finishing with a layer of aubergines.

6. Cover and bake for 40 minutes.

7. Cool for 5 minutes. Tip off any excess liquid. Turn out and serve hot with the remaining tomatoes which have been thinned to the consistency of a sauce with a little stock.

Puddings

Chocolate and Chestnut Mousse Cake

SERVES 4-6

140g/5oz semi-sweet dark chocolate
45g/1¹/₂oz unsalted butter
225g/8oz tinned unsweetened chestnut purée
4 eggs
55g/2oz caster sugar
1 egg white
icing sugar
lightly whipped double cream

1. Line the base and sides of a 20cm/8 inch diameter, 5cm/2 inch deep, cake tin with greaseproof paper. Lightly oil the paper and dust it out with flour.

2. Melt the chocolate and butter in a small saucepan. Tip into a bowl and beat well until smooth.

3. Set the oven to 180°C/350°F/gas mark 4.

4. Sieve the chestnut purée into the chocolate and butter mixture.

5. Separate the eggs. Whisk the egg yolks with the sugar until thick, pale and mousse-like. Add this to the chocolate and chestnut mixture and mix well.

6. Whisk the egg white until stiff but not dry. Fold into the chocolate mixture. Pour into the prepared cake tin.

7. Bake for 50 minutes. Leave in the tin to set and cool for 5 minutes. Turn out and dust lightly with the icing sugar. Serve the whipped double cream separately.

LIQUEUR MUSCAT

Cold Lemon Soufflé

SERVES 4
juice and rind of 2 large lemons
15ml/3 teaspoons of agar-agar (see NOTE I,
page 36)
3 eggs
140g/5oz caster sugar
150ml/¼ pint double cream, lightly whipped

For the decoration:
whipped double cream
wafer-thin lemon slices
browned nibbed almonds

1. Measure the lemon juice. Make it up to 150ml/¼ pint with water. Soak the agar-agar in the lemon juice in a small saucepan, for 5 minutes. Dissolve over a gentle heat until clear. This may well take 20 minutes.

2. Separate the eggs. Place the yolks, lemon rind and sugar in a mixing bowl and whisk together with an electric mixer (or with a balloon whisk or rotary beater with the bowl set over a saucepan of simmering water). Whisk until very thick. If whisking by hand over hot water, remove from the heat and whisk for a few minutes longer, until the mixture is lukewarm.

3. Fold in the cream. Taste and if too tart, sift in a little icing sugar; if too bland, add a little more lemon juice. Then whisk the egg whites until stiff but not dry and fold them into the soufflé with a large metal spoon.

4. Boil the agar-agar for 1 minute and carefully fold it in to the lemon souffle mixture. Pour the mixture into a soufflé dish and leave to set in the refrigerator for 2-3 hours. Decorate with rosettes of cream, lemon slices and nuts.

NOTE: This dish can be given a more soufflé-like appearance by tying a double band of oiled paper round the top of the dish so that it projects about 2.5cm/1 inch above the rim, before pouring in the mixture. (The dish must be of a size that would not quite contain the mixture without the added depth given by the paper band.) Pour it in to come about 2.5cm/1 inch up the paper, above the top of the dish. When the soufflé is set, carefully remove the paper and press the almonds round the exposed sides.

SWEET WHITE

Hot Chocolate Soufflé

To make a successful hot chocolate soufflé you must have everything organized before you start to cook and work as quickly as possible. It is quite difficult to do.

SERVES 4
butter, melted
55g/2oz plus 5ml/1 teaspoon caster sugar
110g/4oz dark bitter chocolate
4 egg yolks
30ml/2 tablespoons brandy (optional)
5 egg whites
icing sugar

1. Set the oven to 200°C/400°F/gas mark 6. Preheat a baking sheet. Prepare the soufflé dish by brushing the inside with melted butter and dusting it with 5ml/1 teaspoon caster sugar.

2. Chop the chocolate with a large knife and put it into a bowl over a saucepan of gently simmering water, stirring until the chocolate has completely melted.

3. Beat the remaining sugar and the egg yolks together for 1 minute with a wooden spoon until thick and fluffy. Add the brandy if using. Add the egg-yolk mixture to the chocolate, mixing well – it will thicken slightly.

4. Whisk the whites until they will stand in soft peaks when the whisk is withdrawn from the bowl. Whisk in 5ml/1 teaspoon caster sugar, until stiff and shiny. Gently but thoroughly fold them into the mixture.

5. Turn into the soufflé dish but do not fill more than two-thirds of the dish. Run the handle of a wooden spoon around the top edge of the soufflé mixture. This gives a 'top hat' appearance to the cooked soufflé. Bake on the hot baking sheet for 20-25 minutes.

6. Test by giving the dish a slight shake or push. It if wobbles alarmingly, it needs further cooking; if it wobbles slightly it is ready. Dust with icing sugar and serve at once.

NOTE: When making a soufflé always remove the oven shelf above the soufflé dish, just in case the soufflé rises unexpectedly well!

FORTIFIED SWEET WHITE

Orange Mousse

This is a very low-fat, sugar-free mousse.

SERVES 4-6
150ml/¼ pint water
10ml/2 teaspoons of agar-agar (see NOTE I,
  page 36)
200ml/7 fl oz carton frozen concentrated
  orange juice, defrosted
15ml/1 tablespoon brandy
290ml/½ pint low-fat natural yoghurt
2 egg whites

1. Put the water into a small saucepan. Sprinkle on the agar-agar and leave it to stand for five minutes. Dissolve the agar-agar over a gentle heat; this may take 20 minutes. Boil for 1 minute.

2. Mix together the orange juice, brandy and yoghurt.

3. Whisk the egg whites until they are stiff but not dry. Fold them into the orange base.

4. Fold in the agar-agar – be careful not to overmix. Pour into a glass bowl and leave to set in the refrigerator.

NOTE I: To make orange ice cream, make the mousse as above and freeze until solid. Remove from the freezer 20 minutes before serving.

NOTE II: This mousse should be eaten on the day it is made.

SWEET WHITE

Black Coffee Jelly with Greek Yoghurt

This is a sugar-free jelly and will be a shock to people with a sweet tooth!

SERVES 4
570ml/1 pint black coffee
concentrated apple juice
10ml/2 teaspoons of agar-agar (see NOTE I,
  page 36)
Greek yoghurt

1. Make up the black coffee using freshly ground coffee beans and, while still warm, sweeten to taste with the concentrated apple juice. Leave to cool.

2. Put 150ml/¼ pint of the cool coffee into a small saucepan, sprinkle on the agar-agar and set aside for 5 minutes.

3. Dissolve the agar-agar over a gentle heat. This may take up to 20 minutes. Boil for 1 minute. When warm, pour into the coffee and spoon into suitable small moulds. Refrigerate until set. This will take about 1 hour.

4. Turn the moulds out on to individual plates and place a good dollop of Greek yoghurt on to each plate.

NOTE: This jelly should be eaten on the day it is made.

Bread and Butter Pudding

SERVES 4

2 slices of plain bread
30g/1oz butter
30ml/2 tablespoons currants and sultanas,
*   mixed*
10ml/2 teaspoons candied peel
2 eggs and 1 yolk
15ml/1 rounded tablespoon sugar
290ml/¹/₂ pint creamy milk
vanilla essence
ground cinnamon
demerara sugar

1. Spread the bread with butter. Cut into quarters. Then arrange in a shallow ovenproof dish, buttered side up, and sprinkle with currants, sultanas and candied peel.

2. Make the custard: mix the eggs and yolk with the sugar and stir in the milk and vanilla essence.

3. Pour the custard carefully over the bread and leave to soak for 30 minutes. Sprinkle with ground cinnamon and demerara sugar.

4. Heat the oven to 180°C/350°F/gas mark 4.

5. Place the pudding in a roasting pan of hot water and cook in the middle of the oven for about 45 minutes or until the custard is set and the top is brown and crusty.

NOTE: The pudding may be baked without the bain-marie (hot-water bath) quite successfully, but if used it will ensure a smooth, not bubbly custard.

SWEET WHITE

Queen's Pudding

SERVES 4
290ml/¹/₂ pint milk
15g/¹/₂oz butter
30g/1oz caster sugar for the custard
60ml/4 tablespoons fresh white breadcrumbs
grated rind of 1 lemon
2 eggs
30ml/2 tablespoons raspberry jam, warmed
110g/4oz caster sugar for the meringue

1. Set the oven to 180°C/350°F/gas mark 4.

2. Heat the milk and add the butter and sugar. Stir until the sugar dissolves, then add the breadcrumbs and lemon rind.

3. Separate the eggs. When the bread-crumb mixture has cooled slightly, mix in the egg yolks. Pour into a pie dish and leave to stand for 30 minutes.

4. Bake for 25 minutes or until the custard mixture is set. Remove and allow to cool slightly.

5. Turn down the oven to 150°C/300°F/ gas mark 2. Then carefully spread the jam over the top of the custard. (This is easier if you melt the jam first.)

6. Whip the egg whites until stiff. Whisk in 10ml/2 teaspoons of the meringue sugar. Whisk again until very stiff and shiny and fold in all but half a teaspoon of the remaining sugar.

7. Pile the meringue on top of the custard and dust the top lightly with the reserved sugar. Then bake until the meringue is set and straw coloured (about 10 minutes).

NOTE I: This is particularly good served hot with cold whipped cream.

NOTE II: When making a meringue mixture with a powerful electric mixer, gradually add half the sugar when the whites are stiff. Whisk again until very shiny and then add the remaining sugar and whisk lightly until just incorporated.

SWEET WHITE

Crème Brûlée

Crème brûlée is best started a day in advance.

SERVES 4-5
290ml/½ pint double cream
1 vanilla pod or 5ml/1 teaspoon vanilla essence
4 egg yolks
15ml/1 tablespoon caster sugar

For the topping:
caster sugar

1. Put the cream with the vanilla pod into a pan and heat up to scalding point, making sure it does not boil. Remove the vanilla pod.

2. Set the oven to 170°C/325°F/gas mark 3.

3. Beat the egg yolks with the caster sugar and when light and fluffy, stir in the warm cream. Place the mixture in the top of a double saucepan, or in a bowl over a pan of simmering water, on a gentle heat. Stir all the time until the custard coats the back of the spoon. If using vanilla essence, add it now.

4. Pour the custard into an ovenproof serving dish, place in a roasting pan half-filled with hot water and bake for 12 minutes to create a good skin on top. Refrigerate overnight. On no account break the top skin.

5. Next day heat the grill.

6. Sprinkle the top of the custard with a

5mm/¼ inch even layer of caster sugar. To do this, stand the dish on a tray or large sheet of greaseproof paper and sift the sugar over the dish and tray or paper. In this way you will get an even layer. Collect the sugar falling wide for re-use.

7. When the grill is blazing hot, put the custard under it, as close as you can get it to the heat. The sugar will melt and caramelize before the custard underneath it boils. Watch carefully, turning the custard if the sugar is browning unevenly.

8. Allow to cool completely before serving. The top should be hard and crackly.

9. To serve: crack the top with the serving spoon and give each diner some custard (which should be creamy and barely set) and a piece of caramel. Crème brûlée is also good made in individual ramekin dishes. In this event, bake the custard for only 5 minutes.

NOTE: If making crème brûlée for more than 4 or 5 people, either make in individual ramekin dishes or in more than one large dish.

FORTIFIED SWEET WHITE

Almond Dacquoise with Apricot Purée

SERVES 6
5 egg whites
pinch of salt
large pinch cream of tartar
285g/10oz caster sugar
110g/4oz ground almonds
290ml/¹/2 pint double cream

For the purée:
225g/8oz fresh apricots, halved and stoned
sugar to taste

1. Preheat the oven to 140°C/275°F/gas mark 1.

2. Line 2 baking sheets with bakewell paper and mark a 22.5cm/9 inch diameter circle on each.

3. Whisk the egg whites, with a pinch of salt and the cream of tartar, until stiff, then add 40ml/2¹/2 tablespoons of the sugar. Whisk again until very stiff and shiny.

4. Fold in the rest of the sugar. Fold in the ground almonds.

5. Divide the mixture between the 2 baking sheets and spread the meringue to the correct size.

6. Bake for 1 hour. Cool slightly, remove from the bakewell paper and leave to become completely cold.

7. While the meringues are baking, make the apricot purée. Put the apricots into a saucepan with 30ml/2 tablespoons sugar and enough water to come halfway up the apricots. Cook slowly, stirring occasionally, until the apricots are tender.

8. Process the poached apricots with enough of the liquid to make a thick purée. Taste and add extra sugar if required. Cool.

9. Whip the cream. Sandwich the cake together with half the cream mixed with the apricot purée. Decorate the top of the dacquoise with rosettes of cream.

NOTE: When making a meringue mixture with a powerful electric mixer, add half the sugar when the whites are stiff. Whisk again until very shiny and then add the remaining sugar and whisk lightly until just incorporated.

SWEET WHITE

Pavlova

SERVES 4-6
4 egg whites
pinch of salt
225g/8oz caster sugar
5ml/1 teaspoon cornflour
5ml/1 teaspoon vanilla essence
5ml/1 teaspoon white wine vinegar or lemon juice
290ml/1/2 pint double cream, lightly whipped
30g/1oz roughly chopped walnuts
450g/1lb fresh pineapple, cored and cut into
  cubes

1. Set the oven to 140°C/275°F/gas mark 1.

2. Put a sheet of silicone paper on a baking sheet.

3. Whisk the egg whites with a pinch of salt until stiff. Gradually add the sugar, beating until you can stand a spoon in the mixture.

4. Add the cornflour, vanilla and vinegar or lemon juice.

5. Pile the mixture on to the prepared baking sheet, shaping to a flat oval or a circle 3cm/11/2 inches thick. Bake for about 1 hour. The meringue is cooked when the outer shell is pale biscuit coloured and hard to the touch. Remove carefully and gently peel off the paper.

6. When quite cold, spoon on the whipped cream and sprinkle on the fruit and nuts.

NOTE: Any fruits in season can be substituted for nuts and pineapple.

SWEET WHITE

Eve's Pudding

SERVES 4
butter for greasing
675g/11/2lb cooking apples
150ml/1/4 pint water
160g/51/2oz sugar
grated rind of 1 lemon
30g/1oz butter
1 small egg, beaten
55g/2oz self-raising flour
pinch of salt
15ml/1 tablespoon milk

For the crust:
45g/11/2oz butter

1. Set the oven to 200°C/400°F/gas mark 6. Butter a pie dish.

2. Peel, core and slice the apples and place in a heavy saucepan with the water, 110g/4oz sugar and half the lemon rind. Stew gently until just soft, then tip into pie dish.

3. Cream the butter until soft and beat in the remaining sugar. When light and fluffy, add the beaten egg by degrees and mix until completely incorporated. Then sift the flour with the salt and fold it into the butter and egg mixture.

4. Add the remaining lemon rind and enough milk to bring the mixture to a dropping consistency. Spread this over the apple. Bake in the oven for about 25 minutes or until the sponge mixture is firm to the touch and has slightly shrunk at the edges.

SWEET WHITE

Apple Charlotte

SERVES 4
1kg/2lb apples
85g/3oz sugar
30ml/2 tablespoons apricot jam
15g/¹⁄₂oz butter
8 slices stale, medium-sliced crustless bread
110g/4oz melted butter

For the apricot glaze:
45ml/3 tablespoons apricot jam
60ml/4 tablespoons water

1. Core and slice the apples and put them into a heavy pan. Add the sugar and cook, without water, until very soft. Boil away any extra liquid and push through a sieve. Whisk in the apricot jam.

2. Butter a charlotte mould or deep cake tin.

3. With a pastry cutter stamp one piece of bread into a circle to fit the bottom of your mould or tin and cut it into six equal-sized triangles. Cut the remaining bread into strips.

4. Set the oven to 200°C/400°F/gas mark 6.

5. Dip the pieces of bread into the melted butter. Arrange the triangles to fit the bottom of the mould and arrange strips in overlapping slices around the sides.

6. Spoon in the apple purée and fold the buttery bread back over it.

7. Bake for 40 minutes. Allow to cool for 10 minutes.

8. Meanwhile, make the apricot glaze. Put the jam and water into a small heavy pan and heat, stirring occasionally, until warm and completely melted.

9. Turn out the pudding: invert a plate over the mould and turn the mould and plate over together. Give a sharp shake and remove the mould.

10. Brush the charlotte with the apricot glaze and serve with cream or custard.

NOTE: This looks a little clumsy but tastes delicious.

SWEET WHITE

Chocolate Roulade

SERVES 6

5 eggs
140g/5oz caster sugar
225g/8oz dark sweetened chocolate, roughly
  chopped
75ml/3 fl oz water
5ml/1 teaspoon strong instant coffee
290ml/¹⁄₂ pint double cream
icing sugar

To prepare the tin:
oil, flour, caster sugar

1. Take a large roasting pan and cut a double layer of greaseproof paper slightly bigger than it. Lay this in the tin; don't worry if the edges stick up untidily round the sides. Brush the paper lightly with oil and sprinkle with flour and then caster sugar. Set the oven to 200°C/400°F/gas mark 6.

2. Separate the eggs and beat the yolks and the sugar until pale and mousse-like.

3. Put the chocolate, water and coffee into a thick-bottomed saucepan and melt over a gentle heat. Stir into the yolk mixture.

4. Whisk the whites until stiff but not dry. With a metal spoon, stir a small amount thoroughly into the chocolate mixture, to 'loosen' it. Fold the rest of the whites in gently. Spread the mixture evenly on the paper.

5. Bake for about 12 minutes until the top is slightly browned and firm to touch.

6. Slide the cake and paper out of the roasting pan on to a wire rack. Cover immediately with a damp tea towel (to prevent the cake from cracking) and leave to cool, preferably overnight.

7. Whip the cream and spread it evenly over the cake. Roll up like a Swiss roll, removing the paper as you go. Put the roll on to a serving dish and, just before serving, sift a little icing sugar over the top.

NOTE I: The cake is very moist and inclined to break apart. But it doesn't matter. Just stick it together with the cream when rolling up. The last-minute sifted icing sugar will do wonders for the appearance.

NOTE II: If this cake is used as a Yule log the tendency to crack is a positive advantage: do not cover with a tea towel when leaving overnight. Before filling, flip the whole flat cake over on to a tea towel. Carefully peel off the backing paper, then fill with cream and roll up. The firm skin will crack very like the bark of a tree. Sprigs of holly or marzipan toadstools help to give a festive look. A dusting of icing sugar will look like snow.

FORTIFIED SWEET WHITE

Hazelnut Roulade

SERVES 4-6

3 eggs
55g/2oz caster sugar
15ml/1 tablespoon plain flour
1.25ml/¼ teaspoon baking powder
55g/2oz browned ground hazelnuts
icing sugar
150ml/¼ pint double cream, whipped

1. Set the oven to 180°C/350°F/gas mark 4.

2. Prepare a paper case as for a Swiss roll. It should be the size of a piece of A4 paper. Grease it lightly.

3. Separate the eggs and beat the yolks and the sugar together until pale and mousse-like.

4. Sift the flour with the baking powder and fold it into the egg-yolk mixture along with the nuts.

5. Whisk the egg whites until stiff but not dry and fold into the mixture.

6. Spread the mixture into the prepared paper case.

7. Bake for about 20 minutes until the top is slightly browned and firm to touch.

8. Remove the roulade from the oven and allow to cool, covered with a sheet of kitchen paper.

9. Sprinkle icing sugar on to a piece of greaseproof paper and turn the roulade on to it. Remove the original piece of paper.

10. Spread the whipped cream evenly over the roulade and roll it up like a Swiss roll.

NOTE: Serve the hazelnut roulade with a raspberry coulis, or add fresh fruit to the cream before rolling up the roulade.

RICH SWEET WHITE

Apple and Orange Crumble

SERVES 4
3 oranges
900g/2lb cooking apples
45ml/3 tablespoons demerara sugar
pinch of cinnamon

For the crumble:
170g/6oz plain flour
pinch of salt
110g/4oz butter
55g/2oz sugar

1. Peel the oranges as you would an apple, with a sharp knife, removing all the pith. then cut out the segments leaving behind the membranes.

2. Peel and core the apples. Cut into thick slices. Mix with the orange segments and their juice. Add the sugar and cinnamon. Tip into an ovenproof dish.

3. Set the oven to 200°C/400°F/gas mark 6.

4. Sift the flour and salt into a bowl. Rub in the fat and when the mixture resembles coarse breadcrumbs mix in the sugar. Sprinkle it over the apples and oranges. Bake on a hot baking sheet for 45 minutes or until hot and slightly browned on top.

NOTE: If using wholemeal flour for the crumble topping, use 140g/5oz of melted butter. Instead of rubbing it into the flour, mix briskly with a knife.

SWEET WHITE

Charlotte's Higgledy Piggledy Tart

SERVES 6
walnut pastry made with 225g/8oz flour (see
*   page 150)*
150ml/¹/₄ pint double cream, lightly whipped
290ml/¹/₂ pint crème pâtissière (see page 154)
soft seasonal fruit such as apricots, oranges,
*   plums, kiwis, bananas and strawberries*
apricot glaze (see page 111)

1. Line a flan ring with the pastry. Chill for 30 minutes.

2. Preheat the oven to 375°F/190°C/gas mark 5.

3. Bake the flan case blind for 20 minutes (see note on page 48). Leave to cool.

4. Fold the cream into the almost cold crème pâtissière and pile into the flan case. Spread flat.

5. Prepare the fruit as for a fruit salad and arrange in a higgledy piggledy fashion.

6. Brush or spoon some warm apricot glaze over the top.

SWEET WHITE

Pecan Pie

SERVES 8-10
For the pastry:
225g/8oz plain flour
pinch of salt
140g/5oz butter
10ml/2 teaspoons sugar
30-45ml/2-3 tablespoons cold water

For the filling:
450g/1lb shelled pecan nuts
4 eggs
225g/8oz soft brown sugar
170g/6oz golden syrup
2.5ml/1/2 teaspoon salt
55g/2oz unsalted butter, melted
vanilla essence
30ml/2 tablespoons flour

1. Preheat the oven to 200°C/400°F/gas mark 6.

2. Sift the flour and salt into a bowl. Rub in the butter until the mixture resembles breadcrumbs.

3. Add the sugar and stir in enough water to bind the pastry together.

4. Roll out the pastry and use it to line a 28cm/11 inch flan case. Leave it in the refrigerator for about 30 minutes to relax. (This prevents shrinkage during cooking.)

5. Bake the pastry blind (see note on page 48).

6. Meanwhile, make the filling: chop half the pecan nuts. Whisk the eggs in a large bowl until frothy. Add the sugar, syrup, salt, melted butter and vanilla essence and beat well until thoroughly mixed. Stir in the sifted flour, making sure there are no lumps of flour in the mixture.

7. Scatter the chopped nuts over the cooked pastry case and pour over the filling. Arrange the remaining halved pecan nuts on top.

8. Bake on a baking sheet for 10 minutes and reduce to 170°C/325°F/gas mark 3 for 30-40 minutes or until the centre is just set. Serve warm or cold.

NOTE: The filling will separate slightly when it is cooked but this is normal and tastes quite delicious.

FORTIFIED SWEET WHITE

Tarte Tatin

SERVES 6

For the pastry:
170g/6oz plain flour
55g/2oz ground rice
140g/5oz butter
55g/2oz caster sugar
1 egg, beaten

For the topping:
110g/4oz butter
110g/4oz granulated sugar
900g/2lb cooking apples
grated rind of 1 lemon

1. Set the oven to 190°C/375°F/gas mark 5.

2. To make the pastry: sift the flour and ground rice into a large bowl. Rub in the butter until the mixture looks like breadcrumbs. Stir in the sugar. Add the egg and bind the dough together. Chill while you prepare the filling.

3. To make the filling: melt the butter in a 25cm/10 inch frying pan with a metal handle. Add the granulated sugar and take off the heat. Peel, core and thickly slice the apples. Arrange the apple slices over the melted butter and sugar in the base of the frying pan. Sprinkle on the grated lemon rind.

4. Place the frying pan over a high flame until the butter and sugar start to caramelize. It may take 6-7 minutes and you will be able to smell the change – it is essential that the apples get dark. Remove from the heat.

5. Roll the pastry into a circle 5mm/¼ inch thick, to fit the top of the pan. Lay it on top of the apples and press down lightly. Bake in the oven for 25-30 minutes.

6. Allow to cool slightly, turn out on to a plate and serve warm.

NOTE: If you do not have a frying pan with a metal handle, cook the apples in an ordinary frying pan. Let the butter and sugar mixture become well caramelized and tip into an ovenproof dish. Cover with the pastry and then bake in the oven on a hot baking sheet. It can also be made in a shallow cast-iron dish – if it has handles (or flanges) turning out the Tarte Tatin is quite difficult, but not impossible.

SWEET WHITE

Individual Apple Tarts with Calvados Crème Anglaise

SERVES 4

puff pastry made with 225g/8oz flour (see page 149)
4 dessert apples
caster sugar
egg glaze
apricot glaze (see page 111)

To serve:
15ml/1 tablespoon Calvados
290ml/¹/₂ pint crème anglaise (see page 154), chilled

1. Set the oven to 200°C/400°F/gas mark 6.

2. Roll out the pastry and cut into 4 circles 2mm/¹/₈ inch thick and 12.5cm/5 inches in diameter. Place on a damp baking sheet. With a sharp knife, trace an inner circle about 1cm/¹/₂ inch from the edge of the pastry. Do not cut all the way through the pastry.

3. Peel, core and slice the apples finely and arrange in concentric circles within the border of each pastry tart. Using a sharp knife, mark a pattern on the pastry border.

4. Sprinkle lightly with caster sugar. Brush the pastry rim with egg glaze, taking care not to let it drop down the sides of the pastry.

5. Flour the blade of a knife and use this to 'knock up' the sides of the pastry. Chill for 15 minutes.

6. Bake for 20 minutes. Leave to cool slightly and then brush liberally with warm apricot glaze.

7. Add the Calvados to the well-chilled crème anglaise. Serve the tarts warm with the cold custard.

SWEET WHITE

Poached Pear and Polenta Tart with Soft Cream

SERVES 8
425ml/³/4 pint red wine
55g/2oz sugar
6 whole cloves
3 strips of lemon zest
2.5ml/¹/2 teaspoon ground cinnamon
5 pears

For the pastry:
140g/5oz butter at room temperature
140g/5oz sugar
3 egg yolks
200g/7oz flour
85g/3oz polenta
2.5ml/¹/2 teaspoon salt
extra 15ml/1 tablespoon polenta

For the soft cream:
150ml/¹/4 pint double cream
pear poaching liquid (see recipe)
brandy to taste
few drops of vanilla essence

1. Bring the wine, sugar, cloves, lemon zest and cinnamon to the boil in a medium-sized saucepan and simmer until reduced by about a fifth.

2. Peel the pears and cut them in half. Remove the cores carefully with an apple corer. Slice them into 1cm/¹/2 inch pieces. Put the pear slices into the red-wine mixture and cook carefully over a low heat for approximately 40 minutes or until the pears are tender. Lift them out with a draining spoon and allow them to cool to room temperature.

3. Strain the red wine to remove the lemon zest and cloves. Put the syrup back on the heat, bring to the boil and reduce by half. Some of this will be used to flavour the cream. Set the oven to 200°C/400°F/gas mark 6.

4. To make the pastry: cream the butter and sugar together until well blended. Add the egg yolks one at a time, beating well between each addition. Sift the flour, polenta and salt together and mix into the creamed mixture. Beat until the dough comes together, then knead lightly on a floured surface, adding more flour if necessary, until the pastry is no longer sticky. Rest the pastry in the refrigerator for 20 minutes.

5. Cut the dough in half. Press one half of the dough on to the base and sides of a 22cm/9 inch flan ring. Sprinkle the base with the extra polenta. Spoon the drained pears into the pastry shell.

6. Roll out the remaining dough to 1cm/¹/2 inch thickness. Using a fluted biscuit cutter, cut out as many circles as possible from the dough. Place them on top of the pears, starting on the outside.

Overlap the shapes and continue to cover the top.

7. Bake the tart in the preheated oven for about 30 minutes, covering with greaseproof paper if necessary after 20 minutes.

8. To make the soft cream: whip the double cream until soft peaks are formed. Flavour with some of the poaching liquid, the cognac and the vanilla essence to taste. Serve with the warm tart.

SWEET WHITE

Sablé aux Fraises

This recipe has been adapted from the Roux Brothers' *Pâtisserie*.

SERVES 6
pâte sablé made with 280g/10oz flour (see page 148-9)
675g/1½ lb strawberries, hulled and sliced
425ml/¾ pint raspberry coulis (see page 155)
55g/2oz icing sugar

1. Set the oven to 200°C/400°F/gas mark 6.

2. Divide the dough into 2 pieces to make for easier rolling.

3. Roll out the doughs very thinly and cut into a total of 18 x 10cm/4 inch circles. Bake in the preheated oven for 8 minutes or until a pale golden. Lift on to a wire rack and leave to cool.

4. Cut the strawberries in half and mix them with two-thirds of the raspberry coulis. Leave to macerate.

5. Place a pastry base on 6 pudding plates. Arrange a few macerated strawberries on top. Cover with a second pastry base and more strawberries. Cover with a third piece of pastry and sprinkle generously with icing sugar.

6. Serve the coulis separately or poured around the sablés.

NOTE: Do not assemble this pudding in advance as the pastry will become soggy.

SWEET WHITE

Chocolate Profiteroles

MAKES 30

For the profiteroles:
3-egg quantity choux pastry (see page 150)

For the filling and topping:
570ml/1 pint whipped cream, sweetened with
  15ml/1 tablespoon icing sugar
110g/4oz chocolate, chopped
15g/¹/₂oz butter

1. Set the oven to 200°C/400°F/gas mark 6.

2. Put teaspoons of the choux mixture on a wet baking sheet, about 8cm/3 inches apart.

3. Bake for 20-30 minutes. The profiteroles should swell, and become fairly brown. If they are taken out when only slightly brown, they will be soggy when cool.

4. Make a hole the size of a pea in the base of each profiterole and return to the oven for 5 minutes to allow the insides to dry out. Cool on a wire rack.

5. When cold fill each profiterole with the sweetened cream, using a forcing bag fitted with a small plain nozzle.

6. Put the chocolate into a bowl with the butter and melt over a pan of simmering water.

7. Dip the tops of the profiteroles in the chocolate and allow to cool.

NOTE: If no piping bag is available for filling the profiteroles, they can be split, allowed to dry out, and filled with cream or crème pâtissière when cold, and the icing can be spooned over the top. However, made this way they are messier to eat in the fingers.

FORTIFIED SWEET WHITE

Apple Strudel

SERVES 6

strudel pastry made with 285g/10oz flour (see
page 151) rolled to at least 40 x 60cm/15 x
24 inches

For the filling:
900g/2lb cooking apples
handful of currants, sultanas and raisins
30g/1oz brown sugar
2.5ml/1/2 teaspoon cinnamon
pinch of ground cloves
45ml/3 tablespoons crumbs, browned
grated rind and juice of 1/2 lemon
85g/3oz melted butter
icing sugar

1. Heat the oven to 200°C/400°F/gas mark
6. Grease a baking sheet.

2. Prepare the filling: peel, core and slice
the apples in such a way that they don't
have very sharp corners which will pierce
the delicate pastry, and mix together with
the dried fruit, sugar, spices, crumbs,
lemon rind and juice.

3. Flour a large tea towel. Lay the pastry on
this. If you have not got a big enough piece
of pastry, several smaller ones will do, but
they must be overlapped well.

4. Brush with butter. Then spread the
filling over the pastry evenly. Using the
tea towel to help, roll up as for a
Swiss roll, trying to maintain a fairly close
roll. Lift the cloth and gently tip the
strudel on to the baking sheet. Brush with
melted butter.

5. Bake in the oven until a golden brown
(about 40 minutes). Dust with icing sugar
while still warm.

NOTE: In delicatessens, strudels are
generally sold in one-portion sizes. To
make these you will need leaves of pastry
about 22cm/9 inches square. As they are
easier to handle, they can be lifted without
the aid of the cloth – just flour the table top
to prevent sticking. Bake for 20 minutes.

SWEET WHITE

Turned Mangoes with Limes

I had never seen mangoes served like this until I saw Arabella Boxer's *Sunday Times Cookery Course.* I was immensely impressed as, delicious as they are, mangoes always present the difficulty of how to eat them.

½ mango and 2 lime wedges a head

1. Cut a thick slice as close to the flat stone as possible.

2. Repeat on the other side. (Use the remaining mango flesh for another dish.)

3. With a small, sharp knife, make diagonal cuts through the flesh right down to the skin – be careful not to pierce the skin.

Cut the flesh to give a lattice finish.

Turn mango inside out.

4. Push the skin up in such a way that the mango is domed and can be eaten with a spoon. Serve with lime wedges.

Watermelon Salad

SERVES 6
1 large watermelon
110g/4oz strawberries
15ml/1 tablespoon triple-distilled rose water

To decorate:
white gypsophilla (if available)

1. Cut off the top of the watermelon. Remove as much of the flesh as possible. Discard the seeds and cut the flesh into neat pieces.

2. Hull and halve the strawberries.

3. Mix together the strawberries, watermelon flesh and rose water. Pile back into the watermelon shell and replace the top. Put on a large plate and decorate with the white gypsophilla.

Arranged Fruit Salad

SERVES 4

2 ripe passionfruits
1 large ripe mango
45ml/3 tablespoons orange juice
seasonal fruit, chilled, e.g. 4 kiwi fruits, peeled
*   and sliced, 110g/4oz strawberries, hulled,*
*   110g/4oz black grapes, peeled and halved*
4 sprigs mint

1. Process (but do not liquidize) the passionfruit pulp, mango flesh and orange juice together for 2 minutes.

2. Sieve the purée on to the base of 4 pudding plates so that each one is well flooded.

3. Arrange the prepared fruit in a pretty pattern on each plate. Decorate each with a sprig of mint.

NOTE: If you do not have a food processor, this sauce can be made in a liquidizer if the passionfruit are sieved before 'whizzing'.

Hot Winter Fruit Salad

SERVES 4

450g/1lb good-quality mixed dried fruits, such
*   as prunes, apricots, figs and apples*
cold tea
15ml/1 tablespoon Calvados
60ml/4 tablespoons orange juice
3-4 cloves
1 x 5cm/2 inch piece cinnamon stick
1.25ml/¼ teaspoon mixed spice
pared rind of 1 lemon
1 star anise

1. Soak the mixed dried fruits in the Calvados and enough tea to just cover. Leave overnight.

2. Pour into a saucepan, add the orange juice, cloves, cinnamon, mixed spice, lemon rind and star anise. Bring up to the boil and simmer slowly until the fruits are soft. This will take about 20 minutes.

3. Remove the cloves, cinnamon, lemon rind and star anise. Serve hot or cold.

FORTIFIED SWEET WHITE

Butterscotch Figs

SERVES 4
8 ripe figs
140g/5oz caster sugar
55g/2oz unsalted butter
pinch of ground cinnamon
60ml/4 tablespoons Grand Marnier

To serve:
150ml/¼ pint double cream, lightly whipped

1. Preheat the oven to 150°C/300°F/gas mark 2.

2. Prick the figs with a fork. Place them in a casserole dish and sprinkle over 30g/1oz of the sugar. Add a little water and bake for 30 minutes. Baste the figs occasionally.

3. Meanwhile, melt the butter in a large sauté pan, add 60ml/4 tablespoons water and the sugar and boil until lightly browned. Add the figs, sprinkle with a little ground cinnamon and toss gently with 2 wooden spoons so that they become lightly caramelized all over.

4. Heat the Grand Marnier in a small saucepan and then pour it over the figs to flame.

5. Serve the figs in a little sauce and serve the cream separately.

FORTIFIED SWEET WHITE

Greek Iced Fruit Salad

a selection of fruit: cantaloupe melon, red
*   apples, bananas, black grapes, oranges,*
*   strawberries, cherries, etc.*
lemon juice
crushed ice

1. Put all the fruit, unprepared, into the refrigerator for a few hours to chill well.

2. Prepare the fruit for eating with the fingers, i.e. peel the oranges and break into segments, picking off any pith. Wash, quarter and core the apples and slice, using a stainless steel knife. Break the grapes into bunches of 3 or 4 grapes each. Peel the bananas and cut into largish pieces. Cut the melon into quarters, remove the peel and cut the flesh into fingers. Leave the strawberries whole and unhulled, washing them only if they are sandy. Wash the cherries, leaving the stalks intact.

3. Arrange the fruit attractively on a very well chilled dish and sprinkle with lemon juice. Sprinkle with ice just before serving.

NOTE I: Apples can be peeled of course, but shiny red ones look good unpeeled. And fruit that is liable to discolour, such as bananas, pears and apples, should be cut up shortly before serving.

NOTE II: To crush ice cubes, put them in a strong plastic bag or cloth and beat with a rolling pin.

LIGHT SWEET WHITE

Pears in Red Wine

SERVES 4

150ml/¼ pint water
150ml/¼ pint red wine
110g/4oz sugar
15ml/1 tablespoon redcurrant jelly
pared rind of 1 lemon
pinch of cinnamon or 1 cinnamon stick
4 firm pears
30g/1oz browned almond flakes
140ml/5 fl oz double cream, whipped

1. Place the water, wine, sugar and jelly in a thick-bottomed saucepan and heat gently until the sugar has dissolved. Add the lemon rind and cinnamon. Peel the pears very neatly without removing the stalks. Place upright in the pan and cover with a lid. The pears should be completely covered by the wine and water mixture so choose a tall narrow pan. If this is not possible, wet the pears in the mixture thoroughly and turn them during cooking. Bring the mixture to the boil and then set to simmer slowly for at least 20 minutes. The pears should be a deep crimson colour and very tender. The longer and slower the pears cook the better. (They can even be cooked overnight in an extremely low oven.)

2. Remove the pears from the pan and place in a glass bowl. Reduce the wine liquid by rapid boiling to a syrupy consistency and strain it over the pears. Allow to cool, and then chill. Sprinkle over the browned nuts just before serving and serve the whipped cream separately.

RICH SWEET WHITE

Raspberries and Fromage Blanc with Fresh Figs

This is a low-fat, sugar-free pudding.

SERVES 4

225g/8oz fresh raspberries
concentrated apple juice
60ml/4 tablespoons low-fat fromage blanc
4 ripe figs, cut into quarters

To garnish:
sprigs of mint

1. Liquidize the raspberries with enough water to make a smooth purée. Taste and add a little apple juice to sweeten, if required. Strain and pour on to one side of 4 pudding plates.

2. Mix the fromage blanc with a little water and pour on to the other half of the pudding plates.

3. Marble the fromage blanc and raspberry purée together with a large fork and arrange the figs on top of the sauces. Garnish with the sprigs of mint.

LIGHT SWEET WHITE

Creamed Cheese with Fresh Fruit

This dessert is simple to prepare and is particularly suitable for a buffet party.

SERVES 4-6
225g/8oz cottage cheese
290ml/¹/₂ pint double cream, lightly whipped
55g/2oz icing sugar
2 drops vanilla essence
3 figs, quartered
3 kiwis, peeled and sliced
4 oranges, peeled and segmented

1. Put the cottage cheese into a sieve and drain very well.

2. Push the cheese through the sieve (or process briefly in a processor) and fold in the lightly whipped double cream. Sweeten with the sifted icing sugar and add the drops of vanilla essence.

3. Pile on to a large oval dish and shape into a shallow mound. Arrange the fruit attractively on top of the cheese.

LIGHT SWEET WHITE

Summer Pudding

SERVES 4-6
900g/2lb redcurrants, blackcurrants, blackberries, raspberries and strawberries (or just some of these fruits, mixed)
30ml/2 tablespoons water
170g/6oz sugar
6-9 slices stale white bread

To serve:
double cream, lightly whipped

1. Cook the redcurrants, blackcurrants and blackberries with the water and sugar until just soft but still bright in colour. Add the raspberries and strawberries. Drain off most of the juice and reserve. Then dip slices of the bread into the reserved fruit juice and use it to line a pudding basin.

2. While the fruit is still just warm, pour it into the bread-lined basin. Cover with a round piece of bread dipped in the fruit juice. Tip the remaining juice into a saucepan and reduce, by boiling rapidly, to a syrupy consistency. Leave to cool.

3. Stand the pudding basin on a dish. Press a saucer or plate on top of the pudding and put a 450g/1lb weight on top. Leave in a cool place overnight. Remove the saucer and weight.

4. Invert a serving dish over the bowl and turn both over together. Give a sharp shake and remove the bowl. Spoon over the reserved, reduced fruit juice. Serve the cream separately.

SWEET WHITE

Ice Creams and Sorbets

ICE CREAM is a foam stabilised by freezing much of the liquid (even when frozen some of the liquid is left unfrozen). There are tiny ice crystals composed of pure water and solid globules of milk fat and there are tiny air cells.

The liquid prevents the formation of a solid block. The ice crystals stabilise the foam by trapping air and fat in its structure and if ice creams contain a good proportion of fat they freeze to a smooth creaminess without too much trouble. If they consist of mostly sugar and water or milk they need frequent beating during the freezing process to prevent too large ice crystals forming. In any event the more a mixture is beaten and churned during freezing the more air will be incorporated and the creamier in texture it will be.

The tiny air cells are very important as they break up the solid liquid to make a lighter, softer texture. Ice cream without air would be difficult to serve, scoop or eat.

MAKING AND STORING

AN ICE-CREAM MAKER The best modern method of churning ice cream is with an ice-cream maker with a built-in chiller and electric motor. These machines are expensive, scaled-down versions of the commercial machines used by caterers. Their chief advantages are that they operate independently of the freezer, and are powerful and large enough to churn even a thick mixture to smoothness. The main disadvantages are the expense and the fact that they take up valuable work space when not in use (they are too heavy for cupboard storage).

AN ELECTRIC SORBETIERE is useful if making small quantities of ice cream from a fairly thin mixture – a custard or a syrup. But few are powerful enough to churn a mixture containing solid pieces (such as pieces of meringue or raisins, for example) or thick mixtures made from, say, mashed bananas. Also, sorbetières must be put into a freezer as they have no built-in chilling equipment and care must be taken when setting up the machine that the lead that connects the churn placed in the freezer to the plug on the wall will not be damaged by closing the freezer door, nor prevent the door closing tight.

A FOOD PROCESSOR will not chill the mixture, of course, but it is powerful enough to churn it to smoothness in a few minutes. Freeze the mixture in a shallow tray until solid, then break it up and process the frozen pieces, using the chopping blade, to pale creaminess. Return to the tray and refreeze.

BUCKET CHURNS can be bought with electric motors or with a handle for manual operation. Most have a good large capacity and are reliable and powerful, but they require a supply of ice and of salt. Coarsely crushed ice is packed in layers, sprinkled with coarse salt, between the metal ice-cream container and the outer bucket. The ice-cream in the container is churned steadily by a strong paddle for 25 minutes or so, until the ice cream is thick. It can be left, without fear of melting, in the churn for an hour or so after making.

MIXING ICE CREAMS BY HAND Finally, ice cream can be made without any special equipment. All that is needed is a shallow ice-cube tray or roasting pan, a bowl, and a strong whisk. The ice cream is half frozen in the tray, then tipped into the bowl (which is chilled) and whisked until smooth. This is repeated until icy shards are eliminated.

SUGAR AND FLAVOURINGS Extreme cold inhibits our sense of taste, the tastebuds being too cold to operate effectively. For this reason ice creams must be sweetened or flavoured more than seems right when tasting the mixture at room temperature.

STORAGE

Theoretically, ice cream can be stored for very long periods, but, certainly in a domestic freezer, there is some deterioration. Ice crystals may form on the surface of the ice cream after a week or so, meringue-based ices or ices containing gelatine may become rubbery, and if raw fruit (such as puréed peach) has been used, the colour will change for the worse. For total perfection, ice cream should be eaten the day it is made. But a few days' freezing is acceptable. If ices are frozen for longer periods, and obviously they often will be, poor texture can be rectified by allowing the ice cream to soften slightly, re-whisking it and re-freezing it. Or the frozen mixture can be re-beaten in a processor. If fruit ices are to be stored for longer than a few days, the fruit should be cooked to preserve the colour.

THAWING

Unless the mixture is very soft, it is wise to put it into the refrigerator for half an hour before serving to allow the ice to soften slightly. Or it may be softened sufficiently to scoop into balls, then put into a chilled serving dish and returned to the freezer until needed.

There are three basic methods of making ice cream.

CUSTARD-BASED METHOD In a custard-based ice cream an egg custard is made with flavoured milk. It will need whisking once or twice during freezing.

MOUSSE-BASED PARFAITS In a mousse-based parfait the air that will give the creaminess to the frozen mixture is beaten into the egg base over heat before cooling and freezing. This means that there is no need to churn or beat once the mixture is in the freezer, and it can be poured into a china soufflé dish with a paper collar tied round it so that it looks deceptively like a risen soufflé or an iced soufflé.

MERINGUE-BASED ICE CREAMS These are similar to the mousse-based parfaits, but the air is incorporated into the egg whites, as for meringue, before the flavouring fruit purée is added. The method is suitable for fruit ice creams, where the acidity of the fruit nicely cuts the sweet meringue.

FROZEN YOGHURTS Yoghurt, because it is so low in fat, is not easy to freeze smoothly without the aid of a machine that beats or stirs constantly during freezing. It thaws and melts too fast for the processor method. The addition of large quantities of cream or sugar would make a smoother and more stable mixture but as frozen yoghurt is often served as a healthy alternative to a fattening dessert, such additions would defeat the cook's object.

SORBETS AND GRANITA Sorbets (sherberts or water ices) are made by freezing flavoured syrups or purées. The essential thing is to get the proportions right. Too much sugar and the sorbet will be oversweet, syrupy and too soft to hold its shape. Too little and it will be icy, crystalline and hard. Chefs use a saccharimeter to measure the amount of sugar in a syrup (a 'pese-syrop' to get the desired 37 per cent sugar), but good results can be had if the mixture contains about one-third sugar and two-thirds other ingredients. Once this figure is in the cook's head, he or she can make almost any sorbet with two-parts liquid (unsweetened) and one-part sugar, bringing the syrup slowly to the boil, cooling it, and freezing it, whisking as necessary.

There is no question that a machine gives the best results. If no machine is available the addition of whisked egg whites helps prevent the formation of large ice crystals and slows up melting.

If slightly less sugar is used, and the mixture is forked rather than beaten while freezing, a granita results – a granular, fast-melting sorbet.

The recipes for ice creams assume that you do not have an ice-cream maker – if you do, simply follow the manufacturer's instructions. Light, sweet wines go with most ice creams, particularly Italian Muscato with fruit ices. Also, try sweet sparkling wine or champagne.

Plum or Apricot Ice Cream

SERVES 6
900g/2lb plums or apricots
110/4oz granulated sugar
3 egg yolks
150ml/¼ pint double cream

1. Stew the fruit with 150ml/¼ pint water and 55g/2oz of the sugar. When tender, push both fruit and juice through a nylon or stainless steel sieve. You should have 290ml/½ pint purée. Taste and check for sweetness.

2. Dissolve the rest of the sugar in 150ml/¼ pint water without boiling it. Then boil rapidly 'to the thread'. (To test, take a little syrup out of the pan with a wooden spoon, dip your fingers in cold water and then dip your finger and thumb into the syrup. The syrup should feel very tacky and form short threads when finger and thumb are drawn apart.)

3. Allow to cool for a ½ minute. Beat the egg yolks with a whisk. Pour on the sugar syrup, whisking all the time, until the mixture is thick, pale and mousse-like, and quite cold.

4. Whip the cream until thick but not totally stiff. Add to the fruit purée with the yolk mixture. Turn into an ice tray.

5. Freeze for about 45 minutes or until beginning to freeze around the edges. Remove the ice cream, stir thoroughly and return to the freezer to freeze completely.

6. If the ice cream is not perfectly smooth, tip it into a chilled bowl, beat until smooth and creamy and refreeze.

Raspberry Ice Cream

This ice cream is made with a mousse base.

SERVES 4-6
450g/1lb raspberries
85g/3oz icing sugar
70g/2¹/₂ oz sugar
110ml/4 fl oz water
a little vanilla essence
3 egg yolks
290ml/¹/₂ pint single or double cream
squeeze of lemon

1. Liquidize or crush the raspberries and push through a nylon or stainless steel sieve.

2. Sweeten with the icing sugar.

3. Place the sugar and water in a saucepan and dissolve over a gentle heat.

4. When completely dissolved, boil 'to the thread'. (When a little syrup is put between finger and thumb and the fingers opened, it should form a sticky thread about 2.5cm/ 1 inch long.)

5. Cool for 1 minute. Add the vanilla essence.

6. Pour the sugar syrup on to the egg yolks and whisk until the mixture is thick and mousse-like.

7. Cool and add the cream, fruit purée and lemon juice.

8. Taste for sweetness and add more icing sugar if necessary.

9. Chill, then freeze.

10. If the ice cream is not quite smooth when half-frozen, whisk it once more and return to the freezer.

Rich Vanilla Ice Cream

This ice cream is made with a mousse base.

SERVES 6-8
70g/2½ oz granulated sugar
120ml/8 tablespoons water
1 vanilla pod
3 egg yolks
425ml/¾ pint double or single cream

1. Put the sugar, water and vanilla pod into a saucepan and dissolve the sugar over a gentle heat, stirring.

2. Beat egg yolks well. Half whip the cream.

3. When the sugar has dissolved, bring the syrup up to boiling point and boil 'to the thread'. Allow to cool for 1 minute. Remove the vanilla pod.

4. Whisk the egg yolks and gradually pour in the sugar syrup. Whisk until the mixture is very thick and will leave a trail.

5. Cool, whisking occasionally. Fold in the cream and freeze.

6. When the ice cream is half frozen, whisk again and return to the freezer.

NOTE: To boil to the thread: to test, dip your finger into cold water, then into a teaspoon of hot syrup, which should form threads between your thumb and forefinger when they are drawn apart.

Brown Bread Ice Cream

SERVES 4
110g/4oz brown breadcrumbs
110g/4oz dark brown sugar
2 eggs, separated
290ml/½ pint double cream
150ml/¼ pint single cream
2 drops vanilla essence

1. Set the oven to 200°C/400°F/gas mark 6.

2. Place the breadcrumbs in the oven for 15 minutes or until dry.

3. Mix the sugar and breadcrumbs and return to the oven for a further 15 minutes or until the sugar caramelizes. Remove, allow to cool and crush lightly.

4. Beat the egg yolks, add the creams and fold in the caramelized crumbs. Add the vanilla essence.

5. Whisk the egg whites to soft peaks and fold into the mixture. Freeze until required.

Peach and Banana Ice Cream with Grape Sauce

Yoghurt-based ice-creams inevitably have a crystal-like texture. The more they are whisked, the smoother they become. With an ice-cream machine, however, they will be almost as smooth as other ice creams.

SERVES 4-6
4 ripe peaches
2 bananas
450g/1lb low-fat yoghurt
concentrated apple juice (optional)

For the sauce:
750ml/1¼ pints black grape juice

1. Peel and stone the peaches. Peel and chop the bananas. Then process or liquidize together with the yoghurt until smooth.

2. Taste and sweeten with the apple juice if required (it will taste less sweet once frozen).

3. Place in the freezer until half-frozen. Tip into a chilled bowl and whisk well. Replace in the freezer until half-frozen and whisk again. Freeze again until firm.

4. Meanwhile, put the grape juice into a saucepan and reduce, by boiling, to a quarter of its original quantity.

5. Remove the ice cream 30 minutes before serving with the grape sauce.

Pear Sorbet

SERVES 4
4 ripe William pears
160g/5½ oz caster or icing sugar
juice of 2 lemons
1 egg white, lightly whisked

1. Peel, core and quarter the pears.

2. Put the pears into a saucepan with the sugar and enough water to just cover the pears. Poach gently for 20 minutes.

3. Remove the pears and reduce the cooking liquor by boiling rapidly until thick and syrupy. (Do not let it begin to caramelize.) Purée the pears, sugar syrup and lemon juice together in a liquidizer or food processor.

4. Allow to cool and then freeze.

5. When nearly frozen, fold in the egg white and freeze until firm.

NOTE: If you have a food processor, allow the sorbet to freeze and then defrost until half-frozen. Whizz in the food processor and gradually add the egg white, unwhisked. It will fluff up.

Passionfruit Sorbet

SERVES 6
170g/6oz granulated sugar
425ml/³/₄ pint water
pared rind and juice of 1 lemon
450g/1lb passionfruit pulp (from about 32
*   passionfruits)*
¹/₂ egg white

1. Dissolve the sugar in the water. Add the lemon rind. Boil rapidly for 5 minutes, or until the syrup is tacky. Then sieve the passionfruit pulp and add to the syrup with the lemon juice. Cool.

2. Place in the deep freeze and leave until icy and half-frozen.

3. Tip into a chilled bowl and whisk well. Refreeze until almost solid.

4. Whisk the egg white until very stiff. Tip the sorbet into another chilled bowl and break up. Whisk until smooth and fold in the egg white. Then freeze again until firm.

5. If the ice is not absolutely creamy and smooth, give it one more freezing and whisking.

NOTE: If you have a food processor, allow the passionfruit, syrup and lemon juice to freeze. Defrost slightly and then whisk until soft. Pour the egg white in, through the funnel, whizzing all the time. Freeze until solid.

Brandy Snap Tortes

SERVES 10
brandy snap mixture made with 110g/4oz flour
*   (see page 155)*
450g/1lb plum ice cream, slightly softened
*   (see page 130)*
raspberry coulis (see page 155)
110g/4oz raspberries and blueberries
sprig of fresh mint
icing sugar for dusting

1. Set the oven to 190°C/375°F/gas mark 5. Grease a baking sheet and palette knife.

2. Make the brandy snap mixture, adding an extra 5ml/1 teaspoon ground ginger. Bake the 20 brandy snaps on the baking sheet as in the recipe but lift them, flat, on to a wire rack and leave them to cool and harden.

3. Put a brandy snap 'flat' on to 10 pudding plates. Cover with some of the plum ice cream and flatten slightly. Cover with a second brandy snap flat. Arrange some more ice cream on top of the brandy snaps and cover with a third brandy snap.

4. Pour the raspberry coulis around the tortes.

5. Mix the raspberries and blueberries together. Arrange them on the coulis and decorate with a small sprig of mint.

6. Dust lightly with icing sugar.

Basic
Recipes

STOCKS, SAUCES, DRESSINGS AND DIPS

Court Bouillon

1.14 litre/2 pints water
150ml/¼ pint vinegar
1 carrot, sliced
1 onion, sliced
1 stick celery
12 peppercorns
2 bay leaves
30ml/2 tablespoons salad oil
salt

Bring all the ingredients to the boil and simmer for 20 minutes.

Vegetable Stock

Vegetable Stock can be made from most vegetables.

1. Simply wash and slice about 450-675g/1-1¹/₂lbs of mixed vegetables such as onions, celery, carrots, leeks and peppers.

2. Put into a large saucepan with 10 black peppercorns, 2 large parsley stalks, a sprig of fresh thyme, the zest of 1 lemon and about 1.14/2 pints of water. Bring to the boil slowly. Skim off any scum. Then simmer for 30-40 minutes. Then strain through a fine sieve and use as required.

French Dressing (Vinaigrette)

45ml/3 tablespoons salad oil
15ml/1 tablespoon wine vinegar
salt and pepper

Put all the ingredients into a screw-top jar. Before using, shake until well emulsified.

NOTE I: This dressing can be flavoured with crushed garlic, mustard, a pinch of sugar, chopped fresh herbs, etc., as desired.

NOTE II: If kept refrigerated, the dressing will more easily form an emulsion when whisked or shaken, and has a slightly thicker consistency.

Tomato Dressing

1 tomato
60ml/4 tablespoons oil
15ml/1 tablespoon water
15ml/1 tablespoon tarragon vinegar
small pinch of English mustard
small pinch of sugar

1. Chop the tomato and whizz in a liquidizer with the remaining ingredients.

2. When well emulsified push through a sieve. If the dressing looks as though it might separate add a little very cold water.

Mushroom Sauce

2 handfuls of mixed herbs (tarragon, parsley, chervil)
150ml/¼ pint vegetable stock (see page 136)
220ml/8 fl oz double cream
30g/1oz butter
110g/4oz button mushrooms
110g/4oz oyster mushrooms
salt and pepper

1. Drop the herbs into a pan of boiling salted water. Bring back to the boil and then strain through a sieve. Pour cold water on to the herbs and squeeze out any excess moisture. Put into a liquidizer.

2. Put the stock and cream into a saucepan, bring up to the boil and simmer until a coating consistency is achieved. Pour into the liquidizer and liquidize with the herbs until smooth and green.

3. Melt the butter in a sauté pan and cook the mushrooms until soft and any liquid has evaporated. Add the herb sauce to the pan and reheat. Season with salt and freshly ground black pepper.

Uncooked Pasta Sauce

This sauce should be served on the day after it has been made in order to allow the flavours to develop. It can be served with hot or cold pasta.

6 large tomatoes, finely chopped
1 red onion, finely chopped
2 garlic cloves, finely chopped
60ml/4 tablespoons chopped fresh basil
15ml/1 tablespoon chopped parsley
90ml/6 tablespoons extra virgin olive oil
juice of ½ lemon
salt and freshly ground black pepper

1. Put the tomatoes into a sieve and drain them for 30 minutes.

2. Mix the tomatoes with the onion, garlic and herbs. Add the oil and lemon juice. Season to taste with salt and pepper.

Ginger and Tomato Sauce

This is a very simple sauce that can be used to accompany pasta and vegetable dishes. This quantity fills two sauceboats. Simply process or liquidize together the following ingredients.

400g/14oz canned tomatoes
3 spring onions
10ml/2 teaspoons very finely chopped fresh ginger
1 large garlic clove
30ml/2 tablespoons fresh lime juice
10ml/2 teaspoons caster sugar
1 fresh green chilli, deseeded (under cold running water), and chopped
30ml/2 tablespoons roughly chopped fresh

coriander
salt and freshly ground black pepper

Tomato and Cream Sauce

3 large tomatoes, peeled, deseeded and finely
*   diced*
45ml/3 tablespoons double cream
5ml/1 teaspoon wine vinegar
5ml/1 teaspoon strong Dijon mustard
10 leaves fresh tarragon, finely chopped
15ml/1 tablespoon finely chopped parsley
5ml/1 teaspoon finely chopped chervil
5ml/1 teaspoon cognac
salt, cayenne pepper or Tabasco

1. Put the tomatoes into a sieve and leave to drain.

2. Pour the cream into a bowl and add the mustard, wine vinegar, cognac, salt and cayenne pepper or Tabasco. Whisk until the cream just thickens, but do not let it separate.

3. Add the tomatoes, parsley, tarragon and chervil. Add salt if necessary.

4. Keep in a cold place and serve in a sauceboat.

Salsa Pizzaiola

This recipe has been taken from *A Taste of Venice* by Jeanette Nance Nordio

1 onion, chopped
30ml/2 tablespoons olive oil
3-4 garlic cloves, chopped
1kg/2¼lb tin plum tomatoes
30ml/2 tablespoons tomato purée
10ml/2 teaspoons dried oregano
5ml/1 teaspoon dried basil
1 bay leaf
10ml/2 teaspoons sugar
salt and pepper

1. Fry the onion in the oil until transparent.

2. Add the garlic and cook for a further minute, then stir in the tomatoes with their liquid, the tomato purée, oregano, basil, bay leaf, and sugar. Season with salt and pepper. Bring to the boil and then cook very gently for about 1 hour.

3. Remove the bay leaf and check the seasoning. This sauce should be quite thick and rough but you could purée it if you wish.

Salsa Romesco

290ml/½ pint olive oil
2 green peppers, deseeded and sliced
5 tomatoes, chopped
3 garlic cloves, crushed
1 dried red chilli
20 hazelnuts, roasted and ground
15ml/1 tablespoon white wine vinegar
salt and freshly ground black pepper

1. Heat the oil, cook the peppers, tomatoes, garlic and chilli for 5 minutes.

2. Add the hazelnuts and vinegar, put into

a liquidizer and blend until smooth. Season to taste.

Tomato, Basil and Olive Oil Sauce

55ml/2 fl oz olive oil
1 garlic clove, flattened but not crushed
2 medium tomatoes, peeled, seeded and finely chopped
4 large basil leaves
salt and pepper

1. Place the oil and the garlic in a small saucepan and place over a gentle heat to infuse for a few minutes.

2. Remove the garlic and add the tomatoes and basil. Season with salt and pepper. Serve warm.

Fresh Tomato Sauce

1 large onion, finely chopped
45ml/3 tablespoons oil
10 tomatoes, peeled, deseeded and chopped
salt and freshly ground black pepper
pinch of sugar
150g/¼ pint vegetable stock (see page 136)
5ml/1 teaspoon fresh thyme leaves

1. Cook the onion in the oil for 3 minutes. Add the tomatoes, salt, pepper and sugar, and cook for a further 25 minutes. Add the stock and cook for 5 minutes.

2. Liquidize the sauce and push through a sieve. If it is too thin, reduce, by boiling rapidly, to the desired consistency. Take care: it will spit and has a tendency to catch.

3. Add the thyme. Taste and adjust the seasoning if necessary.

White Sauce

This is a quick and easy basic white sauce.

20g/¾oz butter
20g/¾oz flour
pinch of dry mustard
290ml/½ pint creamy milk
salt and white pepper

1. Melt the butter in a thick saucepan.

2. Add the flour and the mustard and stir over the heat for 1 minute. Draw the pan off the heat, pour in the milk and mix well.

3. Return the sauce to the heat and stir continually until boiling.

4. Simmer for 2-3 minutes and season with salt and pepper.

Mornay Sauce (Cheese Sauce)

20g/¾oz butter
20g/¾oz flour
pinch of dry English mustard
pinch of cayenne pepper

290ml/¹/₂ pint milk
55g/2oz Gruyère or strong Cheddar cheese, grated
15g/¹/₂oz Parmesan cheese, grated
salt and pepper

1. Melt the butter and stir in the flour, mustard and cayenne pepper. Cook, stirring, for 1 minute. Draw the pan off the heat. Pour in the milk and mix well.

2. Return the pan to the heat and stir until boiling. Simmer, stirring well, for 2 minutes.

3. Add all the cheese, and mix well, but do not re-boil.

4. Season with salt and pepper as necessary.

Parsley Sauce

290ml/¹/₂ pint creamy milk
slice of onion
good handful of fresh parsley
4 peppercorns
1 bay leaf
20g/³/₄ oz butter
20g/³/₄ oz flour
salt and pepper

1. Put the milk, onion, parsley stalks (but not leaves), peppercorns and bay leaf in a saucepan and slowly bring to simmering point.

2. Lower the temperature and allow the flavour to infuse for about 10 minutes.

3. Melt the butter in a thick saucepan, stir

in the flour and cook, stirring, for 1 minute.

4. Remove from the heat. Strain in the infused milk and mix well.

5. Return the sauce to the heat and stir continuously until boiling, then simmer for 2-3 minutes. Taste and season.

6. Chop the parsley leaves very finely and stir into the hot sauce.

Soubise Sauce

For the soubise:
30g/1oz butter
60ml/4 tablespoons water
225g/8oz onions, very finely chopped
60ml/4 tablespoons cream

For the béchamel sauce:
20g/³/₄ oz butter
bay leaf
20g/³/₄ oz flour
290ml/¹/₂ pint milk

1. To make the soubise, melt the butter in a heavy pan. Add the water and the onions and cook very slowly, preferably covered with a lid to create a steamy atmosphere. The onions should become very soft and transparent, but on no account brown. Add the cream.

2. Now prepare the béchamel: melt the butter, add the bay leaf and flour and cook, stirring, for 1 minute. Draw off the heat, and stir in the milk. Return to the heat and bring slowly to the boil, stirring continuously. Simmer for 2 minutes. Remove the bay leaf and mix with the soubise.

NOTE: This sauce can be liquidized in a blender or pushed through a sieve if a smooth texture is desired.

Green Sauce

Delicious with cauliflower and pasta.

30g/1oz butter
30g/1oz flour
290ml/1/2 pint milk
salt and pepper
bunch of watercress, trimmed and chopped

1. Melt the butter and stir in the flour. Cook, stirring, for 1 minute.

2. Remove from the heat, pour in the milk. Mix well. Return to the heat and stir continuously until boiling. Simmer for 2 minutes.

3. Add the watercress to the sauce. Cook for 1 minute. Taste and season as required.

4. Liquidize the sauce thoroughly. Do not keep it warm for too long – the colour dulls.

English Egg Sauce

3 hardboiled eggs
45g/1 1/2oz butter
45g/1 1/2oz flour

570/1 pint vegetable stock (see page 136)
45ml/3 tablespoons cream
60ml/4 tablespoons chopped fresh parsley
salt and freshly ground black pepper

1. Using a stainless steel knife, chop the eggs roughly.

2. Melt the butter in a saucepan. Stir in the flour and cook for 1 minute. Remove from the heat, add the stock and mix well.

3. Return the sauce to the heat and stir continuously until boiling, then simmer for 2-3 minutes, stirring occasionally.

4. Just before serving, add the remaining ingredients and season to taste. This sauce does not keep warm well.

Mayonnaise

2 egg yolks
salt and pepper
5ml/1 teaspoon pale mustard
290ml/1/2 pint olive oil, or 150ml/1/4 pint each
  olive and salad oil
squeeze of lemon juice
15ml/1 tablespoon wine vinegar

1. Put the yolks into a bowl with a pinch of salt and the mustard and beat well with a wooden spoon.

2. Add the oil, literally drop by drop, beating all the time. The mixture should be very thick by the time half the oil is added. Beat in the lemon juice.

3. Resume pouring in the oil, going rather

more confidently now, but alternating the dribbles of oil with small quantities of vinegar.

4. Add salt and pepper to taste.

NOTE: If the mixture curdles, another egg yolk should be beaten in a separate bowl, and the curdled mixture beaten drop by drop into it.

Green Mayonnaise

bunch of watercress
290ml/¹/₂ pint mayonnaise (see page 141)
salt and freshly ground black pepper

1. Pick over the watercress to remove stalks and yellowed leaves. Wash well. Dry thoroughly and chop very finely.

2. Add to the mayonnaise and season to taste.

NOTE: Cooked and very well drained spinach can be used instead of watercress.

Elizabeth Sauce

This sauce was invented by the staff at the Cordon Bleu School for the Coronation in 1953 and has become a classic.
1 small onion, chopped
10ml/2 teaspoons oil
10ml/2 teaspoons curry powder
2.5ml/¹/₂ teaspoon tomato purée
45ml/3 tablespoons water
1 small bay leaf

60ml/4 tablespoons red wine
salt and pepper
10ml/2 teaspoons apricot jam
1 slice lemon
5ml/1 teaspoon lemon juice
290ml/¹/₂ pint mayonnaise (see page 141)
30ml/2 tablespoons double cream

1. Cook the onion gently for 10 minutes in the oil.

2. Add the curry powder and fry gently for 1 minute.

3. Add the tomato purée, water, bay leaf, wine, salt, pepper, jam, lemon slice and juice and simmer for 8 minutes.

4. Strain the mixture, pushing as much as possible through the sieve. Leave to cool.

5. When cold, use this sauce to flavour the mayonnaise to the desired strength.

6. Half-whip the cream and stir into sauce.

NOTE: This sauce is also delicious made with Greek yoghurt instead of mayonnaise.

Rémoulade Sauce

150ml/¹/₄ pint mayonnaise (see page 141)
5ml/1 teaspoon Dijon mustard
7ml/¹/₂ tablespoon finely chopped capers
7ml/¹/₂ tablespoon finely chopped gherkin
7ml/¹/₂ tablespoon finely chopped fresh
   tarragon or chervil

Mix all the ingredients together.

NOTE: Rémoulade sauce is a mayonnaise with a predominantly mustard flavour. The other ingredients, though good, are not always present.

Tartare Sauce

150ml/¼ pint mayonnaise (see page 107)
15ml/1 tablespoon chopped capers
15ml/1 tablespoon chopped gherkins
15ml/1 tablespoon chopped fresh parsley
1 shallot, finely chopped
squeeze of lemon juice
salt and pepper

Mix everything together. Taste and add salt or pepper as necessary.

NOTE: Chopped hardboiled eggs make a delicious addition.

Easy Hollandaise Sauce

This sauce is fairly foolproof. It takes at least 10 minutes to make.

45ml/3 tablespoons wine vinegar
6 peppercorns
1 bay leaf
blade of mace
30ml/2 tablespoons water
1 egg
2 egg yolks
110g/4oz melted unsalted butter
lemon juice
salt

1. Put the vinegar, peppercorns, bay leaf and mace in a small saucepan and reduce by boiling until only 15ml/1 tablespoon remains. Take the pan off the heat, remove the solid ingredients and add the water.

2. Put the eggs and yolks into the pan. Whisk, off the heat, until thick and fluffy.

3. Return to a gentle heat and, whisking continuously, slowly add the melted butter. Keep whisking, removing from the heat if the sauce gets more than warm, until the sauce is a thick emulsion. This may take up to 10 minutes. Remove from the heat and add lemon juice and salt to taste.

Hollandaise Sauce

45ml/3 tablespoons wine vinegar
6 peppercorns
1 bay leaf
blade of mace
2 egg yolks
salt
110g/4oz softened unsalted butter
lemon juice

1. Place the vinegar, peppercorns, bay leaf and mace in a small heavy saucepan and reduce by simmering to 15ml/1 tablespoon.

2. Cream the egg yolks with a pinch of salt and a nut of butter in a small bowl. Set in a bain-marie on a gentle heat. With a wooden spoon beat the mixture until slightly thickened, taking care that the water immediately around the bowl does not boil. Mix well.

3. Strain on the reduced vinegar. Mix well. Stir over the heat until slightly thickened. Beat in the softened butter bit by bit, increasing the temperature as the sauce thickens and you add more butter, but take care that the water does not boil.

4. When the sauce has become light and thick take it off the heat and beat or whisk for 1 minute. Taste for seasoning and add lemon juice, and salt if necessary. Keep warm by standing the bowl in hot water. Serve warm.

NOTE: Hollandaise sauce will set too firmly if allowed to get cold and it will curdle if overheated. It can be made in larger quantities in either a liquidizer or a food processor: simply put the eggs and salt into the blender and blend lightly. Add the hot reduction, allow to thicken slightly. Set aside. When ready to serve, pour in warm melted butter, slowly allowing the sauce to thicken as you pour.

Herby Hollandaise Sauce

1 shallot, finely chopped
30ml/2 tablespoons chopped fresh tarragon
30ml/2 tablespoons chopped fresh chervil or
*   parsley*
60ml/4 tablespoons wine vinegar
6 peppercorns
1 bay leaf
3 large egg yolks
170g/6oz unsalted butter
pinch of salt
pinch of cayenne

lemon juice

1. Put the shallot, half the tarragon and chervil, the wine vinegar, peppercorns and bay leaf into a small saucepan and simmer until the liquid is reduced to about 15ml/1 tablespoon.

2. Cool slightly and strain into a small pudding basin. Add the egg yolks and mix well.

3. Fit the basin over a saucepan of water, making sure that the water does not touch the bottom of the basin. (Alternatively, set the basin in one end of a roasting tin full of water. Place the empty end of the tin over enough heat to make the water bubble only in that area, leaving the water immediately around your basin hot but not bubbling.) Get the water under and around the bowl to simmering point, stirring the egg yolk mixture with a wooden spoon all the time. Allow to thicken slightly and then gradually add the butter, a teaspoon at a time. The trick is to add the next small blob of butter only when the last one is safely absorbed without curdling. The mixture must stay warm enough for the egg yolk to thicken slightly but must never boil or it will curdle.

4. When all the butter is absorbed you should have a sauce the consistency of soft mayonnaise. Add salt, cayenne and lemon juice (very little) to taste. Stir in the remaining herbs.

5. Serve in a warmed sauce boat.

NOTE: See the note at the end of hollandaise sauce for cooking larger quantities.

Beurre Blanc

225g/8oz unsalted butter
15ml/1 tablespoon chopped shallot
45ml/3 tablespoons wine vinegar
45ml/3 tablespoons water
salt, white pepper
squeeze of lemon

1. Chill the butter then cut it in 3 lengthways, then across into thin slices. Keep cold.

2. Put the shallot, vinegar and water into a thick-bottomed sauté pan or small shallow saucepan. Boil until about 30ml/ 2 tablespoons remain. Strain and return to the saucepan.

3. Lower the heat under the pan. Using a wire whisk and plenty of vigorous continuous whisking, gradually add the butter, piece by piece. The process should take about 5 minutes and the sauce should become thick, creamy and pale – rather like a thin hollandaise. Add salt, pepper and lemon juice.

Saffron Beurre Blanc

3 shallots, finely chopped
240ml/8 fl oz dry white wine
110g/4oz butter, chilled and cubed
15ml/1 tablespoon double cream
salt and white pepper
good pinch of saffron, steeped in 30ml/
* 2 tablespoons hot water for 30 minutes*

15ml/1 tablespoon lemon juice

1. Put the shallots and wine into a saucepan and simmer until reduced by one-third.

2. Add the butter, bit by bit, whisking all the time. Add the cream, salt, pepper and saffron. Sharpen the flavour with a very little lemon juice.

Pesto Sauce

2 garlic cloves
2 large cups basil leaves
55g/2oz pinenuts
55g/2oz fresh Parmesan cheese, finely grated
150ml/¼ pint olive oil
salt

In a liquidizer or mortar, grind the garlic and basil together to a paste. Add the nuts, cheese, oil and plenty of salt. Keep in a covered jar in a cool place.

NOTE: Pesto is sometimes made with walnuts instead of pinenuts, and the nuts may be pounded with the other ingredients to give a smooth paste.

Parsley Pesto

2 garlic cloves
1 large handful freshly picked parsley, roughly
* chopped*
30g/1oz blanched almonds
150ml/¼ pint olive oil
55g/2oz Cheddar cheese, finely grated

1. Process or liquidize the garlic and parsley together to a paste.

2. Whizz in the nuts, then add the olive oil slowly with the motor still running. Whizz in the cheese quickly.

3. Keep in a covered jar in a cool place.

Mustard Sauce

90ml/6 tablespoons oil
30ml/2 tablespoons wine vinegar
15ml/1 tablespoon Dijon mustard
15ml/1 tablespoon chopped dill
salt and pepper

Put all the ingredients together in a screw-top jar. Cover and shake until well emulsified.

Red Pepper Sauce

1 onion, finely chopped
15ml/1 tablespoon sunflower oil
2 tomatoes, peeled and deseeded
1 red pepper, peeled (by singeing over a flame), deseeded and cut into strips
1 garlic clove, crushed
1 bouquet garni
90ml/6 tablespoons water
salt and pepper

1. Cook the onion in the oil until just beginning to soften. Add the tomatoes, red pepper, garlic and bouquet garni. Add the water and season lightly. Then cover and cook slowly for 20 minutes.

2. Liquidize until smooth and push through a sieve. Chill.

Black Bean Sauce

45ml/3 tablespoons fermented black beans
2 spring onions, chopped
15ml/1 tablespoon sunflower oil
1 garlic clove, sliced
2.5 cm/1 inch piece root ginger, peeled and sliced
30ml/2 tablespoons soy sauce
30ml/2 tablespoons sherry
5ml/1 teaspoon sugar
290ml/½ pint water
10ml/2 teaspoons sesame oil

1. Wash the beans again and again.

2. Heat the oil in a saucepan, add the spring onions, garlic and ginger and cook for 1 minute.

3. Add the soy sauce, sherry, beans, sugar and water. Bring slowly to the boil, then simmer for 15 minutes to allow the flavour to infuse. Then stir in the sesame oil. Use as required.

Apple Sauce

450g/1lb cooking apples
finely grated rind of ¼ lemon
45ml/3 tablespoons water
10ml/2 teaspoons sugar
15g/½ oz butter

1. Peel, quarter, core and slice the apples.

2. Place in a heavy saucepan with the lemon rind, water and sugar. Cover with a lid and cook very slowly until the apples are soft.

3. Beat in the butter, cool slightly and add extra sugar if required. Serve hot or cold.

Avocado Dip

2 avocados, mashed
1 garlic clove, crushed
15ml/1 tablespoon chopped fresh chives
225g/8oz cream cheese
juice of 1/2 lemon

Combine everything together, beat well, and season to taste.

Cream Cheese Dip

225g/8oz cream cheese
15ml/1 tablespoon soured cream
30ml/2 tablespoons chopped fresh chives
salt and freshly ground black pepper
a little milk

Mix the cream cheese with the soured cream and chives, season with salt and pepper and add enough milk to bring the dip to the required consistency.

Blue Cheese Dip

225g/8oz blue cheese
1 shallot, very finely chopped

15ml/1 teaspoon vinegar
salt and freshly ground black pepper
60ml/4 tablespoons soured cream

Beat the cheese with a wooden spoon and mix in the shallot and vinegar. Season with salt and pepper and beat in the soured cream.

PASTRIES

Shortcrust Pastry (Pâte Brisée)

170g/6oz plain flour
pinch of salt
85g/3oz butter or margarine
very cold water

1. Sift the flour with the salt. Rub in the fat until the mixture looks like coarse breadcrumbs.

2. Add 30ml/2 tablespoons water to the mixture. Mix to a firm dough, first with a knife, and finally with one hand. It may be necessary to add more water, but the pastry should not be too damp. (Though crumbly pastry is more difficult to handle, it produces a shorter, lighter result.)

3. Chill, wrapped, for 30 minutes before using. Or allow to relax after rolling out but before baking.

Rich Shortcrust Pastry

170g/6oz plain flour
pinch of salt
100g/3½oz butter

1 egg yolk
very cold water

1. Sift the flour with the salt. Rub in the butter until the mixture looks like breadcrumbs.

2. Mix the yolk with 30ml/2 tablespoons water and add to the mixture.

3. Mix to a firm dough, first with a knife, and finally with one hand. It may be necessary to add more water, but the pastry should not be too damp. (Though crumbly pastry is more difficult to handle, it produces a shorter, lighter result.)

4. Chill, wrapped, for 30 minutes before using, or allow to relax after rolling out but before baking.

NOTE: To make sweet rich shortcrust pastry, mix in 15ml/1 tablespoon caster sugar once the fat has been rubbed into the flour.

Pâte Sablée

285g/10oz flour
pinch of salt
225g/8oz butter, softened
110g/4oz icing sugar, sifted
2 egg yolks

2 drops vanilla essence

1. Sift the flour on to a board with the salt. Make a large well in the centre and put the butter in it. Place the egg yolks and sugar on the butter with the vanilla essence.

2. Using the fingertips of one hand, 'peck' the butter, yolks and sugar together.

3. When mixed to a soft paste, draw in the flour and knead lightly until the pastry is just smooth.

4. If the pastry is very soft, chill before rolling or pressing out to the required shape. In any event the pastry must be allowed to relax for 30 minutes before baking, either before or after rolling out.

Puff Pastry

225g/8oz plain flour
pinch of salt
170-226g/6-8oz butter
150ml/¹/4 pint icy water

1. If you have never made puff pastry before, use the smaller amount of butter: this will give a normal pastry. If you have some experience, more butter will produce a lighter, very rich pastry.

2. Sift the flour with a pinch of salt. Rub in 30g/1oz of the butter. Add the icy water and mix with a knife to a doughy consistency. Turn on to the table and knead quickly until just smooth. Wrap in polythene or a cloth and leave in the refrigerator for 30 minutes to relax.

3. Lightly flour the table top or board and roll the dough into a rectangle about 10 x 30cm/4 x 12 inches long.

4. Tap the butter lightly with a floured rolling pin to get it into a flattened block about 9 x 8cm/3¹/2 x 3 inches. Put the butter on the rectangle of pastry and fold both ends over to enclose it. Fold the third closest to you over first and then bring the top third down. Press the sides together to prevent the butter escaping. Give it a 90-degree anti-clockwise turn so that the folded, closed edge is on your left.

5. Now tap the pastry parcel with the rolling pin to flatten the butter a little; then roll out, quickly and lightly, until the pastry is 3 times as long as it is wide. Fold it very evenly in 3, first folding the third closest to you over, then bringing the top third down. Give it a 90-degree anti-clockwise turn so that the folded, closed edge is on your left. Again press the edges firmly with the rolling pin. Then roll out again to form a rectangle as before.

6. Now the pastry has had 2 rolls and folds, or 'turns' as they are called. It should be put to rest in a cool place for 30 minutes or so. The rolling and folding must be repeated twice more, the pastry again rested, and then again given 2 more 'turns'. This makes a total of 6 turns. If the butter is still very streaky, roll and fold it once more.

Martha Stewart's Walnut Pastry

225g/8oz plain flour
pinch of salt
110g/4oz butter
140g/5oz ground walnuts
45g/1½ oz sugar
beaten egg

1. Sift the flour and salt into a bowl. Rub in the butter until the mixture resembles coarse breadcrumbs. Add the walnuts.

2. Stir in the sugar and add enough beaten egg (probably half an egg) to just bind the mixture together. Knead lightly. Chill before use.

NOTE: If you have a food processor, simply beat all the ingredients together until lightly combined. Chill before use.

Choux Pastry

85g/3oz butter
220ml/7 fl oz water
105g/3¾ oz plain flour, well sifted
pinch of salt
3 eggs

1. Put the butter and water together in a heavy saucepan. Bring slowly to the boil so that by the time the water boils the butter is completely melted. Immediately the mixture is boiling really fast, tip in all the flour and draw the pan off the heat.

2. Working as fast as you can, beat the mixture hard with a wooden spoon: it will soon become thick and smooth and leave the sides of the pan. Beat in the salt.

3. Stand the bottom of the saucepan in a basin or sink of cold water to speed up the cooling process.

4. When the mixture is cool, beat in the eggs, a little at at time, until it is soft, shiny and smooth. If the eggs are large, it may not be necessary to add all of them. The mixture should be of a dropping consistency – not too runny. ('Dropping consistency' means that the mixture will fall off a spoon rather reluctantly and all in a blob; if it runs off, it is too wet, and if it will not fall off even when the spoon is jerked slightly, it is too thick.) Use as required.

Provençal Pastry

340g/12oz plain flour
190ml/⅓ pint virgin olive oil
salt
190ml/⅓ pint lukewarm water

1. Sift the flour into a bowl, add the oil, salt and water and mix as quickly and lightly as possible to a smooth dough.

2. Form into a ball, cover with cling film and relax in the refrigerator for half an hour. Use as required.

NOTE: A delicious alternative to the virgin oil is to use a herb and chilli flavoured olive oil (available in specialist shops).

Filo or Strudel Pastry

285g/10oz plain flour
pinch of salt
1 egg
150ml/¼pint water
5ml/1 teaspoon oil

1. Sift the flour and salt into a bowl.

2. Beat the egg and add the water and oil. First with a knife and then with one hand, mix the water and egg into the flour, adding more water if necessary to make a soft dough.

3. The paste now has to be beaten: lift the whole mixture up in one hand and then, with a flick of the wrist, slap it on to a lightly floured board. Continue doing this until the paste no longer sticks to your fingers, and the whole mixture is smooth and very elastic. Put it into a clean floured bowl. Cover and leave in a warm place for 15 minutes.

4. The pastry is now ready for rolling and pulling. To do this, flour a tea towel or large cloth on a table top and roll out the pastry as thinly as you can. Now put your hand (well floured) under the pastry and, keeping your hand fairly flat, gently stretch and pull the pastry, gradually and carefully working your way round until the paste is paper thin. (You should be able to see through it easily.) Trim off the thick edges.

5. Use immediately, as strudel pastry dries out and cracks very quickly. Brushing with melted butter or oil helps to prevent this. Or the pastry sheets may be kept covered with a damp cloth.

NOTE: If the paste is not for immediate use wrap it well and keep refrigerated or frozen. Flour the pastry surfaces before folding up. This will prevent sticking.

PASTA & BATTERS

Egg Pasta

450g/1lb strong flour
pinch of salt
4 eggs
15ml/1 tablespoon oil

1. Sift the flour and salt on to a wooden board. Make a well in the centre and drop in the eggs and oil. Then using the fingers of one hand, mix together the eggs and oil and gradually draw in the flour. The mixture should be a stiff dough.

2. Knead until smooth and elastic (about 15 minutes). Wrap in polythene and leave to relax in a cool place for 1 hour.

3. Roll one small piece of dough out at a time until paper thin. Cut into the required sized noodles.

4. Allow to dry (unless making ravioli), hanging over a chair back if long noodles, lying on a wire rack or dry tea towel if small ones, for at least 30 minutes before boiling. Ravioli is dried after stuffing.

NOTE: If more or less pasta is required the recipe can be altered on a pro-rata basis, for example a 340g/12oz quantity of flour calls for a pinch of salt, 3 eggs and 12ml/1 scant tablespoon of oil.

French Pancakes (Crêpes)

MAKES ABOUT 12
110g/4oz plain flour
pinch of salt
1 egg
1 egg yolk
290ml/¹/₂ pint milk, or milk and water mixed
15ml/1 tablespoon oil
oil for cooking

1. Sift the flour and salt into a bowl and make a well in the centre, exposing the bottom of the bowl. Into this well, place the egg and egg yolk with a little of the milk.

2. Using a wooden spoon or whisk, mix the egg and milk and then gradually draw in the flour from the sides as you mix.

3. When the mixture reaches the consistency of thick cream, beat well and stir in the oil.

4. Add the rest of the milk; the consistency should now be that of thin cream. (Batter can also be made by placing all the ingredients together in a liquidizer for a few seconds, but take care not to over-whizz or the mixture will be bubbly.)

5. Cover the bowl and refrigerate for about

30 minutes. This is done so that the starch cells will swell, giving a lighter result.

6. Prepare a pancake pan or frying pan by heating well and wiping with oil. Pancakes are not fried in fat like most foods – the purpose of the oil is simply to prevent sticking.

7. When the pan is ready, pour in about 15ml/1 tablespoon batter and swirl about the pan until evenly spread across the bottom.

8. Place over heat and, after 1 minute, using a palette knife and your fingers, turn the pancake over and cook again until brown. (Pancakes should be extremely thin, so if the first one is too thick, add a little extra milk to the batter. The first pancake is unlikely to be perfect, and is often discarded.)

9. Make up all the pancakes, turning them out on to a tea towel or plate.

NOTE I: Pancakes can be kept warm in a folded tea towel on a plate over a saucepan of simmering water, in the oven, or in a warmer. If allowed to cool, they may be reheated by being returned to the frying pan or by warming in the oven.

NOTE II: Pancakes freeze well, but should be separated by pieces of greaseproof paper. They may also be refrigerated for a day or two.

Fritter Batter

125g/4¹/2 oz plain flour
pinch of salt
2 eggs
15ml/1 tablespoon oil
285ml/10 fl oz milk

1. Sift the flour with the salt into a bowl.

2. Make a well in the centre, exposing the bottom of the bowl.

3. Put 1 whole egg and 1 yolk into the well and mix with a wooden spoon or whisk until smooth, gradually incorporating the surrounding flour and the milk. A thick creamy consistency should be reached.

4. Add the oil. Allow to rest for 30 minutes.

5. When ready to use the batter, whisk the egg white until stiff but not dry. Fold it into the batter with a metal spoon. Use the batter to coat the food and fry immediately.

SWEET SAUCES

Crème Pâtissière

290ml/¹/₂ pint milk
2 egg yolks
55g/2oz caster sugar
20g/³/₄oz flour
20g/³/₄oz cornflour
vanilla essence

1. Scald the milk. Then cream the egg yolks with the sugar and when pale, mix in the flours. Pour on the milk and mix well.

2. Return the mixture to the pan and bring slowly up to the boil, stirring continuously. (It will go alarmingly lumpy, but don't worry, keep stirring and it will get smooth.)

3. Allow to cool slightly and add the vanilla essence.

Crème Anglaise (English Egg Custard)

290ml/¹/₂ pint milk
15ml/1 tablespoon sugar
1 vanilla pod or few drops of vanilla essence
2 egg yolks

1. Heat the milk with the sugar and vanilla pod and bring slowly to the boil.

2. Beat the yolks in a bowl. Remove the vanilla pod and pour the milk on to the egg yolks, stirring steadily. Mix well and return to the pan.

3. Stir over gentle heat until the mixture thickens so that it will coat the back of a spoon; this will take about 5 minutes. Do not boil. Pour into a cold bowl.

4. Add the vanilla essence if using.

Sugar Syrup

285g/10oz granulated sugar
570ml/1 pint water
pared rind of 1 lemon

1. Put the sugar, water and lemon rind in a pan and heat slowly until the sugar has completely dissolved. Bring to the boil and cook to the required consistency. Allow to cool.

2. Then strain. Keep covered in a cool place until needed.

NOTE: Sugar syrup will keep unrefrigerated for about 5 days, and for several weeks if kept cold.

MISCELLANEOUS

Raspberry Coulis

340g/12oz fresh raspberries
juice of ¹/₂ lemon
70ml/2¹/₂fl oz sugar syrup (see page 154)

Whizz all the ingredients together in a food processor, and push through a conical strainer.

NOTE: If it is too thin, it can be thickened by boiling rapidly in a heavy saucepan. Stir well to prevent it 'catching'.

Brandy Snap Cups

MAKES 8
110g/4oz sugar
110g/4oz butter
110g/4oz or 60ml/4 tablespoons golden syrup
110g/4oz flour
juice of 1 lemon
large pinch of ground ginger

TO SERVE:
whipped cream or ice cream

1. Set the oven to 190°C/375°F/gas mark 5. Grease a baking sheet, palette knife and one end of a wide rolling pin or a narrow jam jar or bottle.

2. Melt the sugar, butter and syrup together. Remove from the heat. Then sift in the flour, stirring well. Add the lemon juice and ginger.

3. Put the mixture on the baking sheet in teaspoonfuls about 15cm/6 inches apart. Bake for 5-7 minutes. They should go golden brown but still be soft. Watch carefully as they burn easily. Remove from the oven.

4. When cool enough to handle, lever each biscuit off the baking sheet with a greased palette knife.

5. Working quickly, shape them around the end of the rolling pin or greased jam jar to form a cup-shaped mould. Then when the biscuits have taken shape, remove them and leave to cool on a wire rack.

6. Serve filled with whipped cream or ice cream.

NOTE I: If the brandy snaps are not to be served immediately they must, once cool, be put into an airtight container for storage. They become soggy if left out. Similarly, brandy snaps should not be filled with moist mixtures like whipped cream or ice cream until shortly before serving, or they will quickly lose their crispness.

NOTE II: Do not bake too many snaps at

one time as once they are cold, they are too brittle to shape. They can be made pliable again if returned to the oven.

Brioche

MAKES 12 SMALL BRIOCHES OR
1 LARGE ONE
25ml/5 level teaspoons caster sugar
30ml/2 tablespoons warm water
225g/8oz flour
pinch of salt
2 eggs, beaten
55g/2oz melted butter, cool
7g/¼oz fresh yeast

For the glaze:
1 egg mixed with 15ml/1 tablespoon water and
   15ml/1 teaspoon sugar

1. Grease a large brioche mould or 12 small brioche tins.

2. Mix the yeast with 5ml/1 teaspoon of the sugar and the water. Leave to dissolve. Sift the flour with a pinch of salt into a bowl. Sprinkle over the sugar. Make a well in the centre. Drop in the eggs, yeast mixture and melted butter and mix with the fingers of one hand to a soft but not sloppy paste. Knead on an unfloured board for 5 minutes or until smooth.

3. Put into a clean bowl, cover with a damp cloth or greased polythene and leave to rise in a warm place until doubled in bulk (about 1 hour). Then turn out and knead again on an unfloured board for 2 minutes.

4. Place the dough in the brioche mould (it should not come more than halfway up the mould). If making individual brioches, divide the dough into 12 pieces. Using three-quarters of each piece, roll them into small balls and put them in the brioche tins. Make a dip on top of each brioche. Roll the remaining paste into 12 tiny balls and press them into the prepared holes. Push a pencil, or thin spoon handle, right through each small ball into the brioche base as this will anchor the balls in place when baking

5. Cover with greased polythene and leave in a warm place until risen to the top of the tin(s). The individual ones will take 15 minutes, the large one about 30 minutes. Set the oven to 200°C/400°F/gas mark 6. Brush the egg glaze over the brioches. Bake the large one for 20-25 minutes, or small ones for 10 minutes

NOTE : If substituting dried for fresh yeast when following a recipe, halve the weight of yeast called for. Dried yeast takes slightly longer to work than fresh yeast, and must first be 'sponged' in the liquid, partly to reconstitute it, partly to check that it is still active. To avoid any beery taste, use rather less than the amount of dried yeast called for and allow a long rising and proving time.

Using too much yeast generally means too fast a rise, resulting in bread with a coarse texture that goes stale quickly. Easy-blend dried yeast is mixed directly with the flour, not reconstituted in liquid first. Sold in small airtight packages, it is usually included in bought bread mixtures.

One 7g/¼oz package usually equals 15g/¹⁄₂₀oz conventional dried yeast or 30g/1oz fresh yeast.

INDEX